CIRCLES OF STRENGTH

COMMUNITY ALTERNATIVES TO ALIENATION

Edited by

HELEN FORSEY

THE NEW CATALYST BIOREGIONAL SERIES

NEW SOCIETY PUBLISHERS

Gabriola Island, BC   *Philadelphia, PA*

Canadian Cataloguing in Publication Data

Main entry under title:
Circles of Strength

(The New catalyst bioregional series;5)
ISBN 1-55092-202-5 (bound)—ISBN 1-55092-203-3 (pbk.)

1. Community. 2. Social networks. 3. Alienation (Social pyschology).
I. Forsey, Helen, 1945-   II. Series
HM131.C57 1992   305   C92-091787-9

® ™-C

Inquiries regarding requests to reprint all or part of *Circles of Strength: Community Alternatives to Alienation* should be addressed to:
New Society Publishers,
PO Box 189, Gabriola Island, BC V0R 1X0, Canada, *or*
4527 Springfield Avenue, Philadelphia, PA 19143, USA

ISBN USA 0-86571-258-1 Hardcover
ISBN USA 0-86571-259-X Paperback
ISBN CAN 1-55092-202-5 Hardcover
ISBN CAN 1-55092-203-3 Paperback

Printed in the United States of America on partially recycled paper using soy-based ink by Capital City Press of Montpelier, Vermont.

Cover and interior art by Maureen Swann.
Cover design by Nancy Adams.

To order directly from the publisher, add $2.50 to the price for the first copy, 75¢ each additional. Send check or money order to:
New Society Publishers
PO Box 189, Gabriola Island, BC V0R 1X0, *or*
4527 Springfield Avenue, Philadelphia, PA 19143

New Society Publishers is a project of the New Society Educational Foundation, a nonprofit, tax-exempt, public foundation in the United States, and of the Catalyst Education Society, a non-profit society in Canada. Opinions expressed in this book do not necessarily represent positions of the New Society Educational Foundation, nor the Catalyst Education Society.

The New Catalyst Bioregional Series

The New Catalyst Bioregional Series was begun in 1990, the start of what some were calling "the turnaround decade" in recognition of the warning that humankind had ten years to turn around its present course, or risk such permanent damage to planet Earth that human life would likely become unviable. Unwilling to throw in the towel, *The New Catalyst's* editorial collective took up the challenge of presenting, in new form, ideas and experiences that might radically influence the future.

As a tabloid, *The New Catalyst* magazine has been published quarterly since 1985. From the beginning, an important aim was to act as a catalyst among the diverse strands of the alternative movement—to break through the overly sharp dividing lines between environmentalists and aboriginal nations; peace activists and permaculturalists; feminists, food co-ops, city-reinhabitants and back-to-the-landers—to promote healthy dialogue among all these tendencies working for progressive change, for a new world. The emerging bioregional movement was itself a catalyst and umbrella for these groups, and so *The New Catalyst* became a bioregional journal for the Northwest, consciously attempting to draw together the local efforts of people engaged in both resistance and renewal from as far apart as northern British Columbia, the Great Lakes, and the Ozark mountains, as well as the broader, more global thinking of key people from elsewhere in North America and around the world.

To broaden its readership, *The New Catalyst* changed format, the tabloid reorganized to include primarily material of regional importance, and distributed free, and the more enduring articles of relevance to a wider, continental audience now published twice yearly in *The New Catalyst's* Bioregional Series—a magazine in book form! Through this new medium, we hope to encourage on-going dialogue among overlapping networks of interest, to solidify our common ground, expand horizons, and provoke deeper analysis of our collective predicament as well as a sharing of those practical, local initiatives that are the cutting edge of more widespread change.

The Bioregional Series aims to inspire and stimulate the building of new, ecologically sustainable cultures and communities in their myriad facets through presenting a broad spectrum of concerns ranging from how we view the world and act within it, through efforts at restoring damaged ecosystems or greening the cities, to the raising of a new and hopeful generation. It is designed not for those content with merely saving what's left, but for those forward-looking folk with abundant energy for life, upon whom the future of Earth depends.

Circles of Strength: Community Alternatives to Alienation is the fifth volume in the series; others include *Turtle Talk: Voices for a Sustainable Future*, (no. 1), *Green Business: Hope or Hoax?* (no. 2), *Putting Power in its Place: Create Community Control!* (no. 3), and *Living with the Land: Communities Restoring the Earth* (no. 4).

The *Bioregional Series* and *The New Catalyst* magazine are available at a discount by subscription. Write for details to: *The New Catalyst*, P.O. Box 189, Gabriola Island, BC, Canada V0R 1X0.

Table of Contents

Acknowledgments

Not everyone has the privilege of putting together a book on a subject of passionate interest to them, and of doing it as a joint project with a circle of friends. The publishers, many of the contributors, and other friends and advisors are part of a widespread but very real community of people working for and celebrating bioregionally based alternatives. To all of them, my sincere thanks; I look forward to our further work together.

Judith and Christopher Plant were wonderful, not only as editors and publishers, but as guides step by step through what was for me the unknown territory of book publishing. Their patience, humor, creativity, intellectual stimulation and good sense are infinitely appreciated. To them and to the other New Society Publishers collective members in Philadelphia, my thanks for their generous support. Maureen Swann, besides delighting me with her artistic interpretations of the themes in the book, coached and supported me throughout the book's gestation and birthing process in ways I shall not enumerate here, but will always gratefully remember. Laird Sandhill inspired me with thoughtful conversations and exciting ideas, and helped tremendously with suggestions from his own experience of community-oriented editing and publishing.

Words are inadequate to convey my appreciation to the authors and interviewees; working with them has been a wonderful experience. Among the many others who gave of their time and energy to help create this book, my special thanks go out to Will Boyce, Jean Christie, Pamela Cross, Gay Doherty, Skye Farris, Alison Gale, Stuart Hill, Charmaine Jones, Judith Marshall, Carlysle McKenzie, Jim Nollman, Jain Peruniak, Karen Seabrooke, and Florence Woolner.

Grateful acknowledgement is also made for permission to reprint previously published articles from the following sources:

"Re-Inhabiting the Earth: Genesis Farm," by Miriam Therese MacGillis, adapted with permission of the author from an article published in *Breakthrough*, the magazine of Global Education Associates, Suite 1848, 475 Riverside Drive, New York, NY 10015.

"Community Ethics: A Word of Warning," by Janet Biehl, excerpted from *Rethinking Ecofeminist Politics*, 1991, with permission from the publisher, South End Press, 116 Saint Botolph Street, Boston, MA 02115.

"Checking Ourselves Out: Power and Leadership in Community Work," a discussion with Lori Marum, Doreen Sterling amd Willy Wolf by Four Worlds Exchange, Vol. 1, No. 4, reprinted with permission from the publisher, Four Worlds Health Promotion Program, Box 143, Pincher Creek, AB T0K 1W0.

"The Burwash Experience," by Joan Newman Kuyek, excerpted from *Fighting For Hope—Organizing to Realize Our Dreams*, 1990, and reprinted with permission from the publisher, Black Rose Books, 3981 Boulevard St. Laurent, Montreal, PQ H2W 1Y5.

"The Death of the Small Commune," by Marge Piercy, reprinted from *Hard Loving*, copyright 1969, Wesleyan University Press, by permission of University Press of New England.

"Eagle's Nest: A Native Community's Response to Violence," by Maureen Miller, adapted with permission of the author from a program prepared for Canadian Broadcasting Corporation's radio series *Open House*, 1992.

"Krutsio: A Desert Metamorphosis," by Adrian Aguirre, adapted with permission of the author from *Principles of Cellularism*, 1990, Federation of Egalitarian Communities, c/o Sandhill Farm, Route 1, Box 155, Rutledge, MO 63563.

"The Michigan Womyn's Worker Village," by We Want the Music Company, excerpted and reprinted with permission from Michigan Womyn's Music Festival Program, 1991, WWTMC, Box 22, Walhalla, MI 49458.

"Daughters of Growing Things," by Rachel L. Bagby and Rachel E. Bagby, adapted with permission of the authors from an article in *Reweaving the World: The Emergence of Ecofeminism*, eds. Irene Diamond and Gloria Fenman Orenstein, 1990, and reprinted with permission from Sierra Club Books, 730 Polk St., San Francisco, CA 94109.

"The Goose Story," author and source unknown.

Foreword

The Geometry of Change

Judith Plant

"It is easy to cut down and destroy. It is much harder to build
up and conserve. But this is what we have done."

—Rameshwar Prasad,
Community Organizer, Village of Seed, Aravali Hills, India.

It is perhaps because human beings are determined to survive that it
is always possible to find a community of people somewhere that can
serve to inspire others. So it is with the villages of Seed and Setwana in
the parched landscape of rural India where the villagers have restored
their communities, after being inspired by Gandhian social reformer
Vinobha Bhave. In thirty years these villages have become models of
self-governance and self-reliance. Writer Jeremy Seabrook describes
daily life in these communities as centering around the common good
of everyone, where even caste boundaries have taken second place to
the collective well-being.

From our First World vantage point, the picture painted of people
living within the constraints of their particular ecosystem, in houses of
slate, stone and earth, and children who greet each other with the words
"peace to the world," seems like a mirage. Here in the western world we
have done a lot of cutting down and destroying, whether trees or each
other, and thus our present situation is now one of painful alienation.
Thoughts of communities like Seed and Setwana seem distant and
beyond reach. And ideas of thirty-year commitments to the same people
and the same place, with all adults taking full responsibility for all of the
workings of community life, are most likely greeted with skepticism.

Unlike land-based cultures which have traditions based on a respect
for all of life on which to build, western civilization has instead done its

best to capitalize on nature, separating people from place for the materialist gain of the few. So while we might yearn for a way of living that centers around caring for each other and the natural world, how we make the leap of faith across this chasm of alienation from life is perhaps the greatest challenge facing modern industrial society. While we know it is possible to live a more integrated life on the basis of examples from other cultures and other parts of the world, it's not immediately clear how we, here in the so-called First World, can get there.

There are clues, however, in what past societies have valued. Though we are currently bereft of a philosophy that works for the benefit of all life, humankind has been brought forward to this point in time, not by war and greed, but more likely as a result of the caring and nurturing of women. It is no accident that Helen Forsey has chosen the circle to represent earth-based feminist community. According to many scholars, including architect Mimi Lobell, the circle has been with our species since the Neolithic and Early Bronze Age when people, grouped in matrilineal and egalitarian clans, took up farming and settled permanently on the land. The sphere illustrates their world view, generated by a newly-centered, stable relationship to the land, and a perception of the world made visible from a particular place. This period of our history revolved around the image of the Great Goddess who *was* the earth and sky, time and space, life and death, being and nonbeing. The circle symbolized the integration of all parts of the whole. For thousands of years people lived in peace, in highly progressive civilizations. (Mimi Lobell, "Spatial Archetypes," from *Revision*, Vol.6, No.2).

Today, we live with "the Grid:" the square world of patriarchy which has no center. Its function is to separate everything into predictable and identical units. As Mimi Lobell continues, this linear world, with its alienating sameness, which reduces people and land into manageable blocks, works well for organizing and controlling masses of people and vast tracts of land (perhaps even the globe). Its raison d'être is to "shape what is organic into machine-like components for the benefit of industry, bureaucracy, the military, and colonial governments." It is to this world that *Circles of Strength* is responding. For the time has come when an increasing number of people are questioning this alienated society that has left them powerless. People in towns, villages, urban neighborhoods and rural communities are actively engaged in experimenting with forms of human organization that reflect more the circle than the square.

There are many expressions of this circling dance of humankind. From a deep desire to survive, we have arranged ourselves in citizens' action groups, roadblocks, intentional communities, village councils, communities defined by gender, grassroots coalitions, temporary affinity groups—the list is almost endless. My own experience comes primarily from intentional community and I remember vividly my first glimpse of what an integrated life would look and feel like. It was a simple image of children learning so much more from experiencing a daily life made rich by a variety of differences among the adults. Yet the communal life, in the end, could not cope with what was at the same time offering so much. Differences, in a culture that insists on sameness, become threatening and divisive.

One of the great eye-openers from my communal experience was that no matter how many times we tried to convince ourselves that we had shed the square grid of post-industrial modern capitalism with all its fear, loneliness and cruelty, in fact we brought that same civilization with us. The truth of the matter is that in all our great efforts to build community, we are constantly being undermined by behavior and systems which make up the present economic, social, and political world we all share and the very people we currently are. We have not been taught what could help us in this great re-organization of human affairs—the redefinition of ourselves in wholistic and integrated communities. In fact, from our intimate relations with each other, to the political arena, most things work against us.

How many community-minded people have had the experience of enthusiastically being part of a group or committee only to find that, in spite of the enthusiasm, the group cannot agree long enough to stay together? Such a situation is so common as to be predictable. And, of course, the danger is that while we are divided, we are most easily subdued. Thus "divide and conquer," a military strategy from the grid mentality, continues to work in the interests of those who grab the spoils and run, and against the best interests of those trying to create a better world. While sometimes this strategy may be part of a public relations scheme, it is also sadly the case that we seem to do it to ourselves. I recently had the nauseating experience of standing next to a public relations man employed by a large forestry company at a public meeting while the community began to show its divisions. He quietly muttered to me, "I told you so," implying that people are incapable of getting themselves organized ....

Oftentimes despairing activists will claim that if only people could see how the system is not working for them, and how those in power are greedily ensuring that more and more of the Earth's riches are in the hands of fewer and fewer people, then surely the people would rise up and things would change? Well, Pogo said it all several years back: "We have met the enemy, and it is us." And once we step outside of the hierarchical mode of decision-making, this comic-strip truth becomes painfully evident. All of us brought up in this culture of alienation suffer from power-over, and many would venture to say that until this insidious behavior is confronted in and among ourselves, we will continue to fail in our great efforts to re-organize.

This is why community building must be a feminist project, and particularly an ecofeminist one. An understanding of how and why women have been subjugated by patriarchy is absolutely fundamental to any rebuilding of human society, or we will delude ourselves and our revolutions will bring us right back to the same behavior with which we started. An ecofeminist perspective enhances feminism's basic message by adding that all of life is seen by the patriarchy to be on this Earth for the use and convenience of the élite. More than just equality is at stake. This culture made sick by power cannot value anything that is not competitive and self-interested because such values as cooperation, sharing, and even love are at odds with the patriarchal determination to turn everything into private property.

As times get tougher, whether economically, socially, or because of political injustice, disease, lack of clean water, or yet another bloody war, we will be increasingly pulled towards each other because we know in our deepest memories that there is the potential for intelligence and strength in familiar groups. If the transformation of patriarchal society succeeds, humanity may have another chance for survival. This requires grappling with alienation in the loving circles of nascent communities. Outwitting our dysfunctional behavior is at the heart of successful community work.

The value of a collection like *Circles of Strength* is that every essay shares some story, anecdote, or piece of wisdom gleaned from this powerful experience of community building. It offers no one "right" vision of community, with the exception that it emphasizes that humanity's future must be one that respects all of life—that in some way draws on the circles from our own ancient story.

This is not a "Polyanna" book about community. Instead of promises of utopia, Helen Forsey—herself a dedicated ecofeminist communitarian—has brought together substantive information on a variety of experiments, both accidental and intentional. It is refreshing to leaf through the pages of this book and find stories from such a diverse range of community experiences. Though not one chapter professes to hold the key ingredients or ultimate experience, each is in itself a circle of strength. Often overlapping, these circles become a tool kit, finally, offering some guidance and wisdom in the struggle for a dignified and healthy way of life.

Drawing by
Maureen Swann

1

Regenerating Community: An Introduction

Helen Forsey

We have just finished planting the peas in the fragrant April earth, and are enjoying the gardeners' sense of delighted satisfaction as the growing season begins again. We share a pot of tea; then, as it's still only midafternoon, a few of us head down the hill to the hammock shop to weave the sturdy hammocks which provide most of the community's cash income. One of the women goes over to the stereo to put on a record—one she especially wants me to hear, she tells me. As I listen to the lyrics, telling of friendship and growth, my heart swells with affection for her and for all the wonderful connections that my years in this community have given me....

Community. A word of many connotations—a word overused until its meanings are so diffuse as to be almost useless. Yet the images it evokes, the deep longings and memories it can stir, represent something that human beings have created and recreated since time immemorial, out of our profound need for connection among ourselves and with Mother Earth.

As social animals, people have always created ways of living together; the theme of community is inherent in human history. But with the advance of patriarchal "civilization" and industrialization, those ways have become increasingly oppressive and harmful to humankind and to the Earth. There is a growing realization now that we must find ways to turn that phenomenon around, to create new communal realities out of our deepest memories and our finest visions.

More and more people are seeking alternatives to the alienation that permeates modern industrial society, where our inter-relationships with

1

other humans, with animals, plants and the Earth itself, are constantly distorted through power hierarchies, prejudices and prescribed roles, through plastic packaging, electronic technology, and layers of concrete and asphalt. Human beings must make major changes in order to get beyond that alienation, to get back into healthy relationships with each other and with the natural environment. The idea behind this book is that building bioregional community is a core part of that healing process.

Communities bring together people and other life forms in complex webs of inter-relationships which mirror those of ecosystems. The concept of bioregionalism situates each community within the natural place or region it inhabits. Just as ecosystems are inherently identified with particular places, human communities, too, are shaped, limited and enabled by the particularities of their bioregions. To the degree that human communities are to become healthy and sustainable, their inhabitants must learn to respect both the potentials and the limitations of the natural environment in which they have their being, as well as their own human possibilities.

*

Many of us in the industrialized world have felt the sickness in "malestream" society killing us, draining our spirits and nullifying our work. We are tired to death of swimming upstream alone; we want to feel grounded, connected, to be able to touch the earth and put down roots. We are searching for simplicity and balance in our lives, for comradeship and challenge in our work and our relationships. We feel a need for hope, for possibilities in the midst of despair, for integrity and wholeness in the struggle against alienation, for stability in place of rootlessness, for nurturing and closeness based on equality and respect, not on obligation and exploitation. These needs dictate the journey that leads us to community.

"People already living in close proximity to each other are looking at the reasons why they are there, and building on their basis of unity."

Some of the communities we find are *intentional*: the people in them have deliberately chosen to live and work together with clear common agreements and ties to a particular place. Others are existing neighborhoods or villages, where people already living in close proximity to each other are looking at the reasons why they are there, and building on their basis of unity. Some are temporary communities formed in the context of political resistance, such as blockades, marches or peace camps. Still others are more geographically dispersed but still close-knit networks of common concern and mutual support.

All these groups are part of what Joan Newman Kuyek calls "a culture of hope." What they are all somehow attempting is to break through the barriers of patriarchal assumptions and the cycles of destruction and despair in order to imagine, remember and create ways of living that correspond to our deepest needs. These efforts, and the connections among them, are the focus of this book.

"Our alienated modern societies must turn again to the wisdom of cultures that integrate and honor both female and male, that understand the need for sustainable, harmonious relations with the Earth and all her creatures."

Modern humanity faces the challenge of learning and integrating the wisdom necessary to reconnect us to our communal roots and to the Earth. The traditional ways of life of native peoples, reflected in their origin stories and in the peaceful development of their societies, embody such wisdom in the context of what could certainly be called *bioregional community*. Although much of that knowledge has been lost or submerged by centuries of colonization and brutality, the essence of those ways has been kept through the vision, courage and sacrifice of generations of native people. Our alienated modern societies must turn again to the wisdom of cultures that integrate and honor both female and male, that understand the need for sustainable, harmonious relations with the Earth and all her creatures. With the guidance of those native people who remember those ways and are willing to share them, we may at last begin to rebuild such a reality. We give thanks for their voices.

Many people working at the grass roots level in community economic development, in native community work, in neighborhood organizing or in community health, know nothing about the existence of intentional communities, let alone about the possible relevance of that experience to their own work. Similarly, there are communitarians who see the intentional community experience as the sum total of what the word "community" means. One of the motivations in shaping this book has been the need to build bridges and weave connections among people working in different kinds of communities, so as to strengthen the foundation for all such work and add to the mutual support, information and inspiration that can be exchanged among us all.

One of the most fascinating and hopeful aspects of the emerging communal ideal is the potential for endless variety. In "Becoming the Forest in Defence of Itself" (*Turtle Talk,* New Society Publishers 1990), Dave Foreman makes the analogy, "If diversity is good for an ecosystem, it's good for a social movement as well," and that certainly applies to communities! *Circles of Strength* is an attempt to honour that diversity, to give readers a taste of the richness of the differences that exist, both among communities, and in any individual community in their cycles over time.

The communities described here are very different from patriarchal capitalism's repeated attempts to define community in its own oppressive terms. They represent, instead, the many kinds of communal experience which are consistent with principles of bioregionalism and equality. Whether or not those terms are used is not important; what counts is whether or not the principles are put into practice. Bioregionalism is the practice that turns phrases like "living in place" and "harmony with nature" into solid, tangible realities. Equality is the practice of mutual respect, without which the concept of community becomes a mockery.

Beyond this, the communities in this book have in common a degree of intentionality, an acknowledgement of problems and complexities, a recognition of what is drawing people together, and a commitment to work to validate and enhance that connectedness.

*

Books can serve as useful tools in the construction of new realities, and the building of bridges from the old to the new. *Circles of Strength* is only one small tool in that construction boom, which seems, at last, to be happening. Beyond the book's scope lies a wealth of knowledge, experience and insights relevant to our purpose. Because the material presented here is best understood in that broader context, it is important now to touch briefly on some of those other ways of seeing and of living bioregional community.

The traditions of dominance have been notoriously bad for the human imagination. The patriarchal penchant for polarization has locked people into either/or modes of thinking which have stifled our creativity and regimented our despair. As we break free and start to build alternatives, we must be ready to expand the horizons of our imaginations, so that we can be open to learning all that is there to learn—all that we *must* learn if we are to survive and to have life abundantly.

Ecosystems by definition involve many species. As we open our minds to understanding communities as ecosystems and ecosystems as communities, this throws new light on what has been a basic theme of human mythology, lifestyles and even science, across cultures and through milennia: kinship and communication with other species. Many people consider their pets to be part of the family, and animals often adopt humans as part of their pack or flock. Findhorn Community in Scotland has become famous for the amazing results of its unique way of relating to vegetables. Biologists like Dian Fossey and Paul Spong have told us about the communal lives of gorillas or whales, suggesting that they might have something to teach us about harmony and cooperation. Surely only the old destructive anthropocentric arrogance would allow us to discount what we can learn from other species, or to continue to exclude them from our concept and practice of community.

"Only the old destructive anthropocentric arrogance would allow us to discount what we can learn from other species, or to continue to exclude them from our concept and practice of community."

In bursting the shackles on our imaginations, fiction can also be a powerful tool to help us conceive of and prepare for the challenges and dilemmas that await us on the road to a better future—as well as those that will likely face us even once we arrive! Fictional utopias often envisage as their basic unit some form of community in which bioregional and feminist values are practised, where racism, sexism and exploitation have no place. This is true of the futurist visions of writers like Marge Piercy (*Woman on the Edge of Time*), Ursula Le Guin (*The Dispossessed*), or Dorothy Bryant (*The Kin of Ata Are Waiting for You*). Books like these have inspired many of us; their radically serious explorations of reality and possibility have provided us with many a hearty feast for thought, and their visions continue to comfort and nourish us as we work at building our communities in the here and now.

Many inspiring modern-day examples of bioregionalism and community are found in grass-roots development initiatives of the poor in countries around the world. The Green Belt movement in East Africa, the Chipko movement and the Sarva Seva farms in India, and small community projects aimed at land-based economic self-sufficiency in rural Jamaica, are only a few of these beacons of hope, many more of which form the subject of *Living With The Land*, the fourth volume in *The New Catalyst* Bioregional Series.

Most people in industrialized countries are completely unaware of the amazing examples of self-sufficient community that arose out of the struggles of certain revolutionary societies to establish models for a better future for their land and their people. In the liberated zones of Mozambique, Guinea-Bissau, Angola and El Salvador during their wars of liberation, revolutionary women and men put astonishing amounts of creative energy into setting up such communities. While still engaged in armed combat, and under the most difficult conditions imaginable, they deliberately focused on integrating appropriate land use, education, health, child care, and production into democratically functioning nuclei of the self-reliant, non-oppressive societies they were—and still are—struggling to build. The stories of these communities have too often been submerged in the accounts of the violence surrounding them, or lost in the tragic aftermaths when disasters—natural, military or political—destroyed the valiant efforts of these people. But the examples are there, and the stories remain to be told.

*

We are in the hammock shop again; a meeting has been called. They have moved the hammock jigs off to the ends of the shop area so as to clear a meeting space in the middle. The agenda is posted on a pillar; it is seared into my brain the moment I look at it. Tensions have been building in the community, and the group needs a scapegoat. That scapegoat is me.

Community, particularly intentional community, has been a bitter experience for many people, and we ignore that fact at our peril. Betrayal, disillusionment, cynicism or despair can be found far too frequently among ex-community people, and not all of it can be attributed to romantic or unrealistic expectations. In mainstream society, perhaps only the family can compare as a focus of such intense desires, frustrations, ideals and contradictions as are found in alternative community.

It is painfully clear that however sincere we may be in our attempts to put our communal ideals into practice, these efforts do not, by themselves, create that better society we are striving for. Noble intentions and community involvement do not automatically free us of the baggage we all carry with us—negative behavior patterns and destructive ways of relating to ourselves, each other and the Earth. Yet to go on relating in those old ways threatens to destroy both our communities and the integrity of the alternatives we have been seeking. This contradiction has spelled the end of countless experiments in collectivity, with some people coming to the tragic—and mistaken—conclusion that such alternatives run counter to human nature.

One of the assumptions underlying this book is that when communal experiments appear to fail, what is at fault is not human nature itself, but rather the stifled and distorted attitudes and alienated behavior that *un*natural and oppressive societies have cultivated. Thus, in order to make possible the fundamental changes in all our relations which alone can form the basis of viable communities, we need to continually develop our understanding of what must be changed and why, as well as our determination and ability to live and interact differently in our daily lives. Without such understanding, the old destructive patterns will tend to dominate our actions, blocking the development of true alternatives, whereas theory alone, without practice, is sterile.

*

To edit a book on community for *The New Catalyst* Bioregional Series was a challenge; I knew that much when I began. I had—and have—high hopes for this book as a tool to help people in many different situations continue to seek out and build those alternatives to alienation that are so urgently needed now in our wounded world. What I did not realize was the extent to which the creation of the book would be not only a fascinating learning experience, but also another part of that community-building process itself.

"Community, particularly intentional community, has been a bitter experience for many people, and we ignore that fact at our peril."

One of the authors told me how the actual work of writing her article brought about a new stage in her group's process of community-building. "It made us start to talk about community again," she said, "refining our ideas about what it is that we're trying to build, and starting to see how we could weave together the different strands of what we're doing." She saw this new collective self-awareness as a source of strength and insight that would help empower them as a community.

Paolo Freire, the great Brazilian popular educator, has developed a concept he calls *praxis*—that self-aware kind of activity which can truly move a person or a group forward, beyond what has existed before, towards liberation, health and empowerment. Praxis is a dialectic in which action and reflection feed into each other and build on one another in a creative and continuing spiral. This spiral process integrating action and reflection is, I think, necessary for building sustainable and life-affirming communities.

My own earliest community experience was as part of a group of nature-loving nonconformists from three continents who throughout the 1960s made their weekend home at a tiny cabin on a pine-crowned rocky outcropping overlooking the Ottawa River. That motley group of rock climbers, hikers and skiers was indeed a community, one that embodied egalitarian and bioregional principles, interdependence, humor and love in a collective experience that profoundly influenced all of us. Yet through all those many seasons, we maintained our community without being aware of, let alone analyzing, the significance of what we were doing. The reflection element of the praxis was missing.

"The communities that the authors speak about are circles of strength, made up of women and men who are committed to building, not a refuge from the "real world," but a home base for carrying on the continuing struggle—nuclei for alternatives that can influence and inspire broader change."

When changes came that threatened the community, therefore, we did not recognize what was happening. We had no way of assessing the impact of the changes on our group life, no guidelines or points of reference to help us determine future directions, no clear commitment to essentials. This meant that the entire experience, though tremendously powerful, was inherently unstable, and, not surprisingly, it failed to survive the altered circumstances.

In the face of the phenomenal crises facing our planet, human communities can no longer afford such a lack of self-awareness. Understanding and responsibility go hand-in-hand. When we put our experiences and our insights together, our visions may yet evolve into holistic collective realities that can resist fragmentation and survive to evolve further, into a continuing future for life on Earth.

So, in our various spots on this planet, groups of our species cluster together again, more or less intentionally, in homesteads, villages, neighborhoods and networks, to forge new ways of living and working together—bioregional communities that can perhaps seed this essential turnaround. And we ask, how can we make the most of these efforts to create a new reality out of our best visions? What pitfalls do we need to watch out for and avoid, so as not to fall back into the old oppressive and Earth-destroying patterns? How can we build, from our scattering of communities, a network of growing strength that can truly help to bring about the enormous cumulative changes the world so desperately needs?

This book addresses these kinds of questions by drawing on the experiences of people who have been acting and reflecting in community for years. The communities that the authors speak about are circles of strength, made up of women and men who are committed to building, not a refuge from the "real world," but a home base for carrying on the continuing struggle—nuclei for alternatives that can influence and inspire broader change.

Community is not a simple solution to the world's problems; we know that simple solutions don't exist in any case. What it may be, though, is humanity's next evolutionary step, giving us the opportunity and the challenge of reconnecting with each other and with our environment, in recognition of what native people refer to as "all our relations." *Circles of Strength* is offered as a contribution to that process.

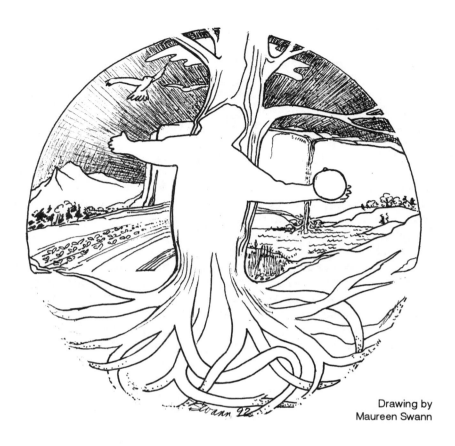

Part One
Crisis and Rediscovery

Communal values and practices that once formed the basis of human life have been eroded by the "power-over" paradigm of modern industrial societies. This fact helps explain the relationship between the current planetary crisis and the personal alienation so many people feel. As we search for healing paths, it is essential that we gain access to what remains of those better ways of living that our species once knew.

Reclaiming and rebuilding the connections that link people with each other and with their environment is the task of bioregional community. Part One explores some memories and visions of what this could mean for us and for our threatened planet.

2

Reinhabiting The Earth: Genesis Farm

Miriam Therese MacGillis

In 1980, Sister Miriam Thérèse MacGillis co-founded Genesis Farm, in Blairstown, New Jersey, as a center for education about the connections between spirituality and global ecological issues. In this article, the educator-farmer-artist reflects on her experience of becoming connected to the physical and spiritual wholeness of the Earth through her work there. The images she weaves of natural communities and their recurring cycles can provide an essential context for our efforts to build communities of human beings in harmony with all other life forms. Miriam MacGillis is a member of the Caldwell, New Jersey, Dominican Sisters, the Catholic community that owns the farm.

Minsi, Minasinniu: *"People of the Stony Country."* Three hundred years ago they inhabited this lush province of the Kitatinny Valley and Ridge—a subregion of the great Appalachian Valley and Ridge that pushes its way from the southern United States to the St. Lawrence Valley in Canada.

Atop the highest hill behind our barn, I can gaze across the ancestral lands of the Minsi. For at least 7000 years, this valley and the Delaware River flowing through it was their home. The river and the people shared an intimate bond and history.

Our farm is one of many that now dominate this gently rolling valley. The Minsi are gone. They were peaceful. Hunting and gathering, planting and hoeing, they satisfied their needs while living in attunement to the natural world. They sought spiritual fulfillment

11

through a close kinship with Manitowuk, whose presence infused these woodlands.

The stony country shaped a way of life for the original people. It is beginning to shape mine. Genesis. Beginning.

Linking Bioregionalism and World Issues

Genesis is an experiment in *reinhabiting* these 140 acres in the Delaware Valley. It is a center where the search for alternative global systems, global spirituality, simplicity of life, land stewardship and sustainable, ecological agriculture all come together.

Over the past ten years, the crisis of hunger and human suffering has worsened. The plight of farmers here and around the planet has intensified. Land ownership has become more centralized. Ecological concerns have been trivialized. These remain tragic symptoms of the national security straitjacket.

They are also symptomatic of the lack of an adequate cosmology. Western education, law, religion, economics and medicine are rooted in an assumption that humans are somehow separate from, and unconnected to, the Earth and its evolutionary journey in the cosmos. This erroneous premise must now be transformed by the realization that humans are a continuation of, and intimately connected to, deeper Earth processes.

An authentic, human-scaled world system must be developed in both its inner and outer dimensions, and in its local and global parameters. It is to these tough issues that Genesis Farm is committed.

In 1979, my Dominican congregation inherited this farm from a family with no prior affiliation to us. The mystery of that gratuitous event continues to evoke in us a deeper understanding of trusteeship and of the responsibility we share for the fate of the Earth.

"A bioregional community is self-propagating, self-nourishing, self-educating, self-governing, self-healing and self-fulfilling."

In the past decade we have struggled to survive, to learn, to be faithful. In the same ten years the North American bioregional movement has emerged. The networks have linked and expanded; the resources have developed and multiplied. For us, the movement has offered viable models, practical plans and concrete tools.

How often we hear "Think globally, act locally." This sense of *local*—of a real physical, defined space—is the core of bioregionalism. As my study of the universe and its evolutionary journey has deepened, so has my awareness of the particular geological and biological history of this place. As I reinhabit this particular place, I experience its connectedness to the inner and outer reaches of the whole Earth.

A series of geological processes molding the Earth's crust has shaped the particular landscape of this bioregion, and centuries of winds and waters continue to modify it. From the last ice-age to the present, a succession of living communities established themselves here, adapting to warming and cooling trends, to geological and soil features, and to the diversity among themselves. Plants, insects and animals learned to form a viable, sustainable community: an eco-system. The long process of biological emergence assured the balanced interaction of the whole, so that the earliest humans to arrive here inserted themselves into a lush and splendid community of life. The region was alive and well. The Minsi learned to live at one with it.

It is into these ever-renewing processes—already enormously altered in the last hundred years without the living wisdom of native elders—that Genesis Farm is now learning to function.

A Bioregional Community

Ecological theologian Thomas Berry describes a bioregional community as "an identifiable geographic area of interacting life systems that is relatively self-sustaining in the ever-renewing process of nature. The full diversity of life-functions is carried out, not as individual or species, or even as organic beings, but as a community that includes the physical as well as organic components of the region. Such a bioregional community is selfpropagating, self-nourishing, self-educating, self-governing, self-healing and self-fulfilling." Each of these six life-functions is evident in the life processes of Genesis Farm.

Self-propagating. Gazing over our fields and woodlots, one could feel secure in the abundance of new vegetation constantly replenishing the old. But the basis of the *evident* signs of life and generativity lie in hidden strata of microscopic scale and monumental significance: *the living universe of the soil.* I am just slowly beginning to understand how the *geological* history of this place has determined the parameters and potentiality for the appropriate life species which have evolved here.

A soil map grids the diversity of terrain, organic composition and water conditions for our entire acreage. The pasture lands, the swamp areas, the forests and cultivated fields each have a unique history and definition. And each of these areas, covered with a garment of living soil, contains a unique and teeming population, an indispensable, extraordinary community of microscopic organisms. Billions of algae, bacteria, fungi and actinomycetes are the *primary* inhabitants of this place. Everything else that lives and grows here is totally dependent on them and their capacity for selfpropagation. Should they disappear, wind and water would quickly erode the fragile skin of soil. The world of green and growing things would shrivel up. The insects, birds and animals would disappear.

Haunting images of starving people fill the evening news, but starving nations continue to give their most fertile land to cash crops planted for export in order to solve their acute balance-of-payment deficits. On any summer day in my own region, supermarkets are stacked with vegetables and fruit from California, Mexico and Central America. Current world trends reflect a more centralized food system. The actual nutritive value of food is diminishing and its appearance is being propped up by cosmetic chemicals. This state of affairs is absurd and violent. Together the movement for global justice and the bioregional movement could reverse these trends.

Self-educating. Thomas Berry says, "To garden is to activate the deepest mysteries of the universe." The process of gardening is an invitation into the journey of the cosmos as it unfolds and reveals itself in a cauliflower. To enter into the *interior* spaces of the natural world is to be confronted with our own arrogance. We must disarm ourselves of so many of our attitudes of dominance or of indifference if we are to discover the Divine.

"A garden is a school. A kitchen, rooted in a garden, governed by the seasons and their appropriate foods, is a school. Learning to become such a school is a process of re-education and discovery."

A garden is a school. A kitchen, rooted in a garden, governed by the seasons and their appropriate foods, is a school. Learning to become such a school is a process of re-education and discovery.

Work, too, is learning. As we continue to work and learn, our workshops will become more integral, more reflective of the self-education that is happening in and through us. As we link our understanding of local and global, we may offer a space where such questions and issues will engage the people who come here with hope and encouragement. Such a learning will force us to sustain both the overwhelming complexities of the global scale and the most intricate details of the local scale. We will need to be contemplatives—at work.

As a farmer, a participant in the food producing cycle, I must learn and revere the wisdom of this process.

Self-nourishing. Several months ago I experienced a moment of profound awareness in a very simple act. The day was cold, the kitchen warm and silent. I was alone enjoying a steaming bowl of vegetarian chili, extremely conscious of its flavors and textures. It occurred to me that this bowl really held rock and soil, minerals and water, and the energy and heat of the stars. All of the ingredients—the beans, onions, garlic, carrots, tomatoes, basil, pepper and oregano—had once been seeds that I inserted into soil.

Now they were all providing me with delight and nourishment. And they would soon become my blood, my bones, my sight, my movement, my thoughts, my prayers. I was overwhelmed by the limitless generosity of the universe and its Creator.

Self-governing. There are fifteen beehives on the farm. As I learn the craft of beekeeping, I am more and more amazed at the monumental work bees do. The internal governance of these creatures—the order observed, their perseverance at work, their community loyalty—is a microcosm of the living order among the life forms on these 140 acres, this bioregion, and the community of bioregions of the planet. Without being aware of their significance, they aid the pollinating abilities of our planet's vegetation. They absorb from it and give back to it.

"We each need to help heal our bioregions. The first step is to heal our own perceptions that fail to see the connections between ourselves and the Earth."

I have also become aware of the precariousness and vulnerability of their lives. The chemical assault on "unwanted" insects and weeds is a major threat to these most beneficial beings. Good local environmental laws do not guarantee their safety. The poisons in our air and water know no geographical borders. Humans must submit to the Earth's internal governance system, or perpetration of these poisons will destroy the natural order which is our life-line.

Self-healing. In spite of our extraordinary medical discoveries, the recuperative powers within the natural world remain largely untapped or foreign to us. There is a legacy of healing in the roots and plants and soil of this place. The Minsi knew and used many of those powers. Some day I hope the farm will explore this realm of healing forces.

Equally important, we need to grasp the relationships that contribute to a healthy planet: soil, air, water, plants, insects—all the living components. And we need to grasp how these are connected to the health of our bodies *and* our spirits.

Our bodies have incredible powers of rejuvenation. So does the Earth. But when the immune system, the recuperative power of the former, breaks down to the degree and magnitude it has, then we must suspect that the immune system of the Earth is in serious difficulty. The Earth is sick. Our air, forests, food, water, birds and whales are sick. We each

---

The Circle—An Invitation

Jaye Borden and Maureen Swann

Consider as you read this that you are entering a circle—a circle made up of everyone who is also reading this book, and everyone who has contributed to it. Visualize yourself together with all these other people, standing in this circle.

Where are we? Is the circle outside on a grassy hillside? Inside, in a gymnasium or classroom? What does the centre of the circle contain—a fire or stone? Or is it simply the space and energy we have collectively formed? What are you bringing to the circle? What are your expectations? How do you feel—excited? shy? vulnerable? confined? safe?

Let's begin in a familiar, time-honored way. Someone in the circle will say their name. You start. Now the next person, and then the next. The circle of names carries a rhythm; soon everyone is saying their name in turn. Eyes meet to connect names with individuals. We may feel tentative, but we have succeeded in grounding the circle. Or, to put it another way, we have claimed our common ground.

Let's hold hands. I will squeeze your hand and you squeeze the next person's, until it passes all around the circle. There. Now something else has been given and received. We are sharing. This is the nature of a circle and the power of creating common ground.

I hold a feather in one hand because I have something to say: we authored this circle because of a recent experience of a

need to help heal our bioregions. The first step is to heal our own perceptions that fail to see the connections between ourselves and the Earth. It is time for the healers among us to go beyond treating only the symptoms of our diseases, and to focus their insights, energies and compassion on the root causes of these symptoms.

Self-fulfilling. Liturgy, celebration, festivals, the making of the beautiful: these flow out of a participation in the grandeur and pathos of the Earth, of this place. Genesis Farm has its own history of struggle and pain, failure and frustration. Our memories are received into the memories of the farm. The tired soil, the decaying trees, the wounded

circle's creative and healing power. In the heat of the Oka crisis between native people and the Canadian Army in the summer of 1990, our community, and the work we had come together to do, were in imminent danger of falling apart. A circle was called, bringing hostile and disparate elements together, demanding relationship and the creation of common ground. In that circle, all our feelings of anger, frustration, confusion and fear were addressed and respected, and offers of support were made. Everyone in that circle felt a spiral of creative energy fill it. It was the beginning of a healing process with a broader base, far beyond that circle itself.

When we ask someone to "share," we should not think that we are asking for something that comes easily and without preparation. We are essentially asking them to do as we have just done in our circle—create relationship or establish common ground. The act of sharing is a conscious, creative one that requires support and safety.

Think about the times you choose to call a circle. Whether it is to facilitate a game, a group orientation, or a conflict resolution, we use the circle's capacity to focus our unique perspectives and to generate collective energy. There is no high or low place within a circle. There is no last or first. It is a great equalizer. Everyone's place is easily recognizable as both unique and similar to our own.

As I pass the feather around this circle, I want to pass it with the hope and faith that we will all allow ourselves to be as children in the circles that we are part of—to have the courage not to know, and the strength to share what we are learning with each other.

deer, the weathered stones, the forgotten Minsi, the exiled wolves, the builders of this house, the family who bequeathed it: we are all links in the ongoing mystery of a creation that is incomplete, finite, and even now struggling to give new birth.

The grandeur of it all! This is what we celebrate and shall continue to celebrate. The universe unfolds in all this struggle. It unfolds in our conscious thought of it. It is in our own reflection that the whole becomes one great conscious act of giving birth. All the components share a single history and a single center. The inner spaces are one space, where dwells the ancient Holy One, the Manito, the One of no name and all names.

Hidden Mysteries

As I write, Genesis is mantled in a deep covering of snow. The world outside is silent, frozen, white. When such a silence descends, I am drawn once again to the ancient, hidden mysteries beneath the ground.

Beneath the frozen crust all living things sleep. Seeds and roots, crickets, microbes, worms and bulbs. It is the law of things. For longer than the longest memory, they have renewed their lives and energies in this communal rite of winter sleep.

"It is good to reflect on the power of small, hidden, insignificant things."

When the last days of autumn yield to this healing sleep, the tiny creatures of the soil and night still sing and dance their journey. And when the very last of their last, last lingering songs falls into silence, that poignant night marks the true time of winter for our region. In some cavernous center, the great Manito breathes the great holy life of the Earth into sleep. Then these hidden, small and insignificant beings rest from the awesome work whereby they sustain the world.

It is good to reflect on the power of small, hidden, insignificant things. It is the way of things.

When the snow has melted and the soil is moist and warmed, a renewal of invisible life shall pound and throb through the marrow of this place. A new generation of rocks and stones shall end their timeless ascent to the surface of our fields. For millions of years they have been pushing, ascending to the top.

How recently I would have greeted their appearance with regret. Another crop of boulders to lug and haul away. And with such effort and sweat—but now, no regret. They are tomorrow's soil. They are treasure of this valley's ancient passage into now.

It is fire I will carry. From field to wall. Fire of a star now frozen into crystal gift. Laid before the sun and stars, these stones will know the force of wind and heat, water and cold. Their fire shall yield and change and break into the crumbled dust of soil. Tomorrow's soil. I carry that from field to wall. I plant them as a row of seeds. Bless them for the journey that will continue long after all the living community of today shall pass away. Worn and broken, they shall yield to life itself, and the hidden, tiny microbes shall break and feed them to the hairs of living roots for the great ascendancy into life. Perhaps they may grow up into wheat, wheat born of fire, fine and strong. Marrow of some future child. Child of the stony country. I will carry the bones of tomorrow's child. *Minsi, Minasinniu.*

3

Rules Which Made
Them Strong

An interview with Jean Trickey

Jean Trickey grew up in Arkansas, where in 1957 she was one of the "Little Rock Nine," the first Black students to integrate Little Rock Central High. In Canada since the late 60s, Jean has continued her history of activism. Homesteading in Northern Ontario, she raised six children and won a five-year battle with the Ontario government for the right to home-school them. Jean is active in the environmental movement and in solidarity with native people, and is deeply committed to non-violence, community-building and social justice. In 1991, she graduated from the Native Human Services program at Laurentian University in Sudbury, and now works in Ottawa.

Helen Forsey: *People look to their communities for mutual support through the vagaries of living. Can you talk some about what that has meant in your life?*

Jean Trickey: I can't really think of a time in my life where I haven't had some kind of support when it was needed. As a child, in the Black community, it was my mother's friends, and her church. I always felt that I had that kind of community support. I guess I always took that support for granted, and assumed that everybody had it. This whole thing of falling through the cracks—there just didn't seem to be that possibility.

In university I was involved in civil rights, so there was that sense of camaraderie with those people who were turning the world upside down. And then coming to Canada as the wife of a draft-dodger, we formed a little group in the midst of Metropolitan Toronto and moved it almost intact into our various back-to-the-land ventures. In our

Northern Ontario community, my husband and I were the first "hippies," but it wasn't long before there they were, coming out of the woodwork. So even in that sixteen-year period, we had incredible support.

In many ways we were trying to get back that kind of communal cooperation, create family in the midst of nothing, create extended family. And in some ways we did it: we supported each other in our miscellaneous adventures, had our babies at home, and people got together and had kind of a cooperative school. It's really hard to home-school—it's all day long, and I don't think a lot of us in our modern world were trained to take care of our kids all the time. It's hard to do all that by yourself, because that stuff is considered by mainstream society to be weird and strange. So you almost have to have at least someone you can bat it off of, or talk to about it.

Then when we had a farm accident, the neighbors just flocked from their place to our place and said, what can we do?

HF: *The neighbors, including those who'd been there for generations?*

Jean Trickey: Everybody, everybody. And we would do the same for them. We understood that whole thing, what community is, what it's about. When you're needed, somehow you've got to come up with something, if it's a box of cookies or whatever it is. Part of that rural mentality is the same kind of Black mentality that we had down home—that that's what you *do*, nobody comes to suggest it, that's just your reaction, it's your response.

"People who live very close to the earth become very keenly aware of the life, the spirit in everything: that it's visible, and hearable, and feelable."

HF: *Do you think that kind of community support has anything to do with a certain sense of adversity, the harshness of the climate and the isolation in the North, the racism of the dominant society in the American South?*

Jean Trickey: I think it's independent of that, because people in the North don't think of it as harsh; really, they don't. And probably in the Black community, it's kind of a combined thing. But I think it's also a cultural thing. Even after 500 years you still come from a communal society, you still have a cultural memory of that.

I always said I didn't have any culture, because it was taken from me. That's blasphemous in a way, but there was nothing I could really point to that was mine specifically. There was music, I guess, but sometimes that music thing can be used as a category, you know: "Oh well, Black people are good at music and that's all they're good at." I guess I've rebelled against being made somebody else's "other," somebody else's definition. I do sing and I am musical, and I love it, but at the same time that's not all I am.

But there was a woman who was working in communities in Africa and Australia, working among colonized people, and she described this Black church in the American South as being very close to a village ceremony, and I hadn't even thought of that. And she said, "Don't ever say you don't have culture, because you do. What happens in the American South is very similar to what happens in Africa."

Being in the Native Human Services program and dealing with a lot of native people was really incredible for me. I'm not native, but I got to see my own cultural memory—the similarity, and there were labels for it and names for different things. In many ways native culture is more intact than say, if we're talking slavery, because there is language, and it's in the same continent, the same place, so in many ways there is a lot of continuity. And it was through that that I got to be able to label my own cultural awarenesses. I got to attach names like "extended family", and now I can attach the concept "basic spirituality" to this whole church thing. So there was another form of community in which I gained lots and was able to pour into myself information, concepts, understandings, clarification of feelings.

It seems to me that people who live very close to the earth become very keenly aware of the life, the spirit in everything: that it's visible, and hearable, and feelable. So I got to understand that aspect of myself. I learned that my particular form of connection to the Earth wasn't weird. Half of us go around thinking we're weird because people keep quiet about those things. But wherever I am, I manage to connect with people and I end up finding other weird people!

"Sometimes in order to experience community, you have to ask for it. Nobody is going to know what your situation is if your door is shut and your curtains drawn."

It doesn't mean that there haven't been times when I've felt myself alone, but at the moment that I reached out, there it was. I think some of it has to do with me, part of my personality is getting involved with other people. I ask a lot of questions of people, and I don't really allow them not to respond to me. And sometimes in order to experience community, you have to ask for it. Nobody is going to know what your situation is if your door is shut and your curtains drawn.

HF: *When you were homesteading up in Northern Ontario, were you ever involved in an intentional community?*

Jean Trickey: The sort of planned community thing where we were going to share everything, some of that didn't quite work. We bought our own land, but we thought that other people could live on it, and other people did live on it. But I turned out not to be a really communal person, because I always had somebody staying there, and I realized that I really was the kind of person who needed personal space. You wouldn't believe it with how many kids I have. Even now I have to fight for that alone time that I require.

HF: *I think that's a crucial issue, particularly in intentional communities; I've experienced it myself, and I keep hearing it from other people. That tells me we need forms of community that respect and allow and encourage that kind of separateness as well as togetherness. We need forms of community that enable an ideal balance for each of us on that spectrum, between a lot of solitary being and a lot of social and communal being, for a range of people, and at different stages in their lives.*

Jean Trickey: Here's what I think. At that time when we were trying to build our communities, there were probably some models based on the surfacey kind of reading about native people in which they lived in a longhouse, so some people thought that you could just throw everybody together. Well, communal people have lots of different other ways, and it's more than just appearance, it's woven into all the traditions and woven in the behaviors, and it takes a long, long time to establish that.

"We need forms of community that enable an ideal balance for each of us on that spectrum, between a lot of solitary being and a lot of social and communal being, for a range of people, and at different stages in their lives."

Another of the things that I learned is this whole idea of non-interference. Native people don't tell other people what to do; they just allow them to do their thing. But as Western dominant people, we tell *everybody* what to do; our reason to *be* is to tell other people how to do everything, OK? So we don't have any of those trainings to keep us from interfering with other people's lives; we've rejected all those social controls that are so-called "primitive" or whatever.

I want to tell you a story about being on a marae in New Zealand. The marae is a large building, it's a traditional religious place, a community hall, decorated with myths and cultural history, all part of the art work in there. The maraes were places of feasts and cultural gatherings.

As visitors from the World Indigenous Conference on Education, we slept 300 people on the upper floor of the marae, and 300 people on the lower floor. Now that is one double sheet covering two pieces of foam, and you share. There are aisles for going in, at people's heads and feet, but there are no aisles between bodies. So there are just rows of people sleeping there. And the funny thing is that it afforded the most privacy that I've ever felt in my entire life. Because that space of your foam is your space, and nobody else invades that space without being asked. If I opened my space, then it became a wonderful space full of people, and we shared, say, six sleeping spaces. At times my space was sat upon or visited by Aborigines who were telling creation stories, and there was a Cree pipe-carrier talking about his dream.

"Part of the reason why we're having to feel our way, every step of the way in community, is because we threw out all those archaic, "primitive" rules by which to live, which were very effective."

The only rules that they gave us were: no eating, no smoking, and no shoes, and that's it. Nothing was written. And yet, the rules, the legislation for that place was feelable, touchable. You knew what you were supposed to do without anybody telling you, by the fact that you were so close together. There was no sex, there was no eating, nobody stepped on anybody. We took those rules into ourselves. Somehow my body created from inside the rules I needed to live there. And *that's* where our governance comes from.

Well, we haven't been trained for that in our society, so when people come, not even as close together as one on top of each other, but even just next door, as in apartment buildings, we erupt into all kinds of craziness. We're compared to mice and lemmings and all that. Because we don't understand the concept, we've rejected all those teachings in our culture which gave us rules to live that way. So part of the reason why we're having to feel our way, every step of the way in community, is because we threw out all those archaic, "primitive" rules by which to live, which were very effective.

In tribal cultures, respect, non-interference means that you recognize people's rights to their boundaries; you don't mess with people. And I think part of the reason why we had so much trouble as hippies trying to set up these communities, was that we wanted to throw away *all* the boundaries, we wanted to just pack into one space and be one big happy family.

HF: *Replace total alienation with total intimacy?*

Jean Trickey: Yeah. Which is impossible. People need to keep their boundaries, where they feel safe. Part of it is that we don't even have anything right now in our culture that allows us to teach our children how to be alone. I come into this society with nothing even to give my kids in terms of what rules to live by. Colonization specifically tried to break all those rules, and that was its primary focus—to prevent people from transferring the rules they had to live by, those rules which made them strong, to their children.

HF: *So how can communities help people to assert themselves, to change their lives, to make things better, and what really is "better?"*

Jean Trickey: People are the experts; they know what it is they need. It's just that nobody listens. But people internalize the dominant view and they feel powerless. Poverty is really a form of social control; it means paucity of resources, including emotional resources. So states of imagination, of daring, of energy, of movement, of excitement, don't often exist at the same time as poverty, because the poverty itself takes so much energy to maintain. Despite my energy and all my wishes to change the world, I think I've changed it less since I've been really poor. This kind of poverty, with children—it dampens my revolutionary zeal. I don't have enough bus fare to go to the revolution, right? It almost costs money to be a revolutionary!

"States of imagination, of daring, of energy, of movement, of excitement, don't often exist at the same time as poverty, because the poverty itself takes so much energy."

What does that mean? Theoretically the revolution is to overturn an intolerable situation, but the inertia that you feel in that intolerable situation is very hard to overcome. The carrot is being held out there and you can't even chase it.

This can go in waves all the way around the world, keeping people busy trying to live so they *can't* live. It can be working in the canefields for not enough money and not raising food on your small plot, to living in a dangerous ghettoized high-rise in Toronto and not being able to walk outside your door. Everybody's in the business of trying to destroy the other person because they can't be engaged in any kind of positive action. So we've sabotaged our society. But if I run into five people who say, "Right on, why don't we do something about this?," then it's going to be a hell of a lot easier.

4

Intentional Community: Pioneering the Connections

Laird Sandhill

One way of practising and sharing an integrated political vision is through intentional community. At this time of planetary crisis, many intentional communities are consciously taking on responsibility for creating history in a new image.

Laird Sandhill is an organic farmer, organizer and group facilitator, and has been a member of Sandhill Farm in Missouri for eighteen years. For most of that time he has been actively involved in networking and organizing through the Federation of Egalitarian Communities and the Fellowship for Intentional Community. He is a key part of the management, editorial and distribution team for the Directory of Intentional Communities. *Here he reflects on the role such communities can play now and in the future.*

M any people have the impression that intentional communities are escapist, or represent a choice which takes members out of the front lines of social change work. Perhaps that's because most intentional communities are rural, and most political attention is focused on the city. It's always been a mystery to me how someone who cares about community can say that it's tangential to their work—that creating community is nice, but not a central thrust of their lives. How can one be drawn only part way into the work of integrating values into daily living? I think of community as being inextricably linked with values of peace, cooperation and equality, and as a responsible, a vital way of dealing with ecological challenges.

Community gives people linked with other individuals the leverage to express themselves and find answers that make sense in a sustainable way. So if you believe in the power of people working together, in the socialness of human beings, then it seems to me you would choose community.

Now, it is a perfectly fine choice to look around you as this realization dawns on you, and decide to cultivate that sense of community in an intentional way wherever you are. Once you realize the power of community and what it can do as an enabler, an empowering avenue, then I think you are intentionally choosing community values, whether or not you do it in what we call an intentional community.

I wonder if it's possible today to be fully engaged in environmental issues—sustainable living, responsible resource use, and not find yourself drawn into issues around oppression and peace. All these issues overlap; they share a common dynamic. There are all kinds of particular entrés to these issues, depending on where your fire is—racism, feminism, disabled people, whatever you've spent the most time thinking about and working on. But it's very hard to say you can fully engage in one without being drawn into the others.

In the analysis of peace, oppression or ecological issues, you need always to consider how your actions impact on others. In community, you must do the work of learning who other people are and how they see things differently, and honoring that, so that you in turn will have your views honored. That is group work, and it is essential for world peace. The same is true for oppression issues, and for how your use of resources limits or enhances others' use of resources. You have to build up from small units; you can't leap to the national or international model without knowing how that works in a group of eight or twelve. Communities I know are doing this work, discovering how groups can get to know each other well enough to function in healthy, non-exploitative ways.

"In community, you must do the work of learning who other people are and how they see things differently, and honoring that, so that you in turn will have your views honored."

Community offers an integrated setting, so that your engagement on these things, your everyday action *is* your life. For a lot of individuals in modern society, this burning fire to work on these issues is a *part* of their lives, or even a central focus, yet a substantial fraction of their lives must be diverted elsewhere, to do the thing that makes them money, or go to the store to buy food to eat. Fragmenting life like that creates a wrenching divisiveness in a person's being. Very few people outside of intentional community are able to arrange their life so that they can follow their heart path—engage on their fire issues—while at the same time paying the bills, creating opportunities for recreation, and providing all the different things that are part of one's package of needs. I think that kind of integration is, in the end, going to be essential to putting out workable models on these issues.

This level of integration is an important way in which intentional community is really different. I know of nothing else like it. You're never done; you're never not at work. Everything you do relates to ecology, equality, peace. That doesn't mean you're constantly conscious of it, but everything can be turned around and analyzed to reveal its relevance to those issues.

I applaud the fact that the communities' movement is an eclectic and diverse group. It is a strength that this integration is offered in many different packages. I don't think that the only legitimate lifestyle choice is intentional community. I do think, though, that there are many, many people who could thrive in community but don't know it's there. As people get deeper into these issues, moving away from the wider culture's models and into more functional and sustainable paths, community will make more sense and be a more attainable step for people to take.

When I came to community, the thing I was looking for was a combination of stimulation and support, a life that was growing. I felt I had slowed down when I left college and got a job; I just wasn't engaged in that exciting a life. It wasn't unpleasant, but I thought, "Gee, I don't want to settle for this!" So I sought out community to try to recapture that sense of growth. And I stayed in community because I did recapture it.

This sense of possibility, this prospect of accelerated growth and stimulation is what keeps me in community. I just don't think I would have turned out anything like the way I have if I hadn't come to community, and sometimes it makes me wince to think what I might have been like without it!

"This sense of possibility, this prospect of accelerated growth and stimulation is what keeps me in community."

Historically, intentional communities have existed mainly as spiritual entities. It isn't until the second half of this century that secular communities—groups that are based on common values other than spiritual ones—start appearing in significant numbers. A good fraction of the spiritual groups, though by no means all, were isolationist, trying to wall off from what they saw as heretical mainstream influence. With the secular groups that doesn't tend to be the case. They tend to be more egalitarian, and temporal in their essential focus. They are still a minority in terms of total communal population, and some of them are politically unfocused, but secular groups in general are much more oriented towards being agents of social change.

Epuyen: A Patagonian Eco-Community

Asociación Lihuen Antu

Lihuen Antu is an association of local inhabitants of Epuyen, in southern Argentina. Our home is the mountain slopes bordering Lake Epuyen
in the Patagonian Forest. Our region has become impoverished due to our country's current dependency and the systematic putting-aside of our concerns by civil servants. Our people, mostly Mapuches, remain submerged in illiteracy and suffer from unemployment and hunger. Many have been forced to migrate to look for jobs far from their families, while those who have stayed face a desperate and uncertain future.

Meanwhile, the Patagonian forests themselves are in danger because of lack of awareness about their important role in this fragile ecosystem. Clearcutting and lack of reforestation, common until a few years ago, had a devastating effect on the region. Thousands of hectares are lost annually to forest fires. Recent monoculture plantations of foreign species such as pine have made it more difficult for the native species to survive; some, like the cipres, radal, pitra, and maiten, are on the brink of extinction.

Several years ago we decided to join together and work for our community with the hope of re-creating social solidarity. Together with local authorities, we began implementing a plan to resolve some of our most urgent problems by promoting subsistence farming, reforestation, local self-sufficiency, and public awareness. For four years, we formed an incredible local government, completely independent of the central powers, tending towards socialist values and with a strong dose of ecology in all our work.

It's from this activist side of things that the network organizations are drawing their strength. We want to get out the word about what we're doing and how we see ourselves as different, as a positive alternative to some of the things we see as ill in the culture. What is going to be the long-term impact of that? There are examples of secular involvement from historic communal groups, like the Harmonists in the nineteenth century who introduced things like public libraries and kindergartens.

Our forest program is called the Lemu Project; *lemu* is the Mapuche word for forest. It was created to promote the importance of the native forests in the life of the region as retainers of the seasonal rains, regulating the flow of rivers and streams and improving irrigation for farming activities. Together with the children and teachers of the local primary school, we started a small tree nursery. The first seeds of native trees were sown, and the children take turns maintaining and watering the seedlings. We also have a series of lectures by a forestry expert on the importance of native forests and local seed harvesting. Through the sale of greeting cards with photographs of our trees and wildlife, we are supporting the native tree nursery and promoting awareness of the threats to our forests, thus ensuring, we hope, their conservation and regeneration.

Since 1987, many fallow lands have been ploughed and wheat sown. The original mills were shut down many years ago, but we obtained a mill to grind our wheat and produce flour and ñaco. Vegetable gardens flourish again, thanks to our distribution of seeds and seedlings; many families now have their basic sustenance. A community carpentry shop uses local materials and represents a partial solution to unemployment, and our yearly crafts festival provides incentive for local cottage industries. To retain ancient wisdom, the Council of Elders was formed; a Youth Council encourages social compromise and participation. Our environmental programs are going even better than we had expected. All this has brought about a revival of hope.

Unfortunately, in 1991, the big political parties formed an alliance to oust us from the local government, and won the election even though our party got more votes than we had four years earlier! But we had foreseen the possibility of defeat, and had our parachutes ready. Our programs continue, and despite the frustration, we are not giving up.

But this is a different time and a different movement, and it's still an unwritten chapter.

If I had to guess, though, I'd say the legacy of today's communities will be the advances we've pioneered in group process and non-hierarchical decision-making. I think, for example, that the process experiences of community will likely play a crucial role in the development of the bioregional movement, and perhaps with the Greens as well.

There has never been as much interest, in at least the last fifteen years, as there is today in either joining or starting a community. Also, because of the maturity of the groups that are involved in the networking, we are now at a place where together we can pool resources and free up individuals in a regular way to do movement work. Existing groups are starting to see that it's not in their best interests just to stay to themselves—that there are considerable benefits in having some kinds of contact with other groups, getting moral and substantive support for what they're doing, and helping others.

I hold a vision of getting enough information out into the wider culture so that everybody is aware of community as an alternative and knows where to go to get more information. It's a question of accessibility, and having it be the kind of thing that kids know about at least by high school—a legitimate, responsible choice. I think of the kibbutzim in Israel as a model of what community could be like here. They are three per cent of the Israeli population—a noticeable minority—yet kibbutzim "graduates" contribute to positions of leadership way out of proportion to their numbers. To me that makes perfect sense. Leadership requires people skilled in group dynamics and democratic decision-making, and in community our lives are full of that. In the not too distant future, I expect North American communities to be able to contribute like that here.

One of the ways that day might be hastened is by focusing on the connections between intentional community and community in the more general sense. The word "community" obviously has a different and broader meaning to most people in our culture. There are many more people and resources devoted to community economic development, for example, than to intentional community networking. While these are very different arenas, there is more in common here than the word community. Lessons of group living undoubtedly have application in the struggles to revivify urban neighbourhoods and rural villages.

A prime challenge for the intentional community movement today is to build better bridges between it and that wider sense of community, enabling much more of the traffic to cross each way. Then, perhaps, the integration will be complete.

5

Women Weave Community

Margo Adair and Sharon Howell

Margo Adair and Sharon Howell are ecofeminists, political activists, teachers, speakers, consultants and writers, who together operate "Tools for Change." Margo, who lives in San Francisco, has done extensive work on the nature of consciousness and integrating politics and spirituality. Sharon works in both the political and academic arenas, organizing in the Detroit area and teaching communications and social movement theory at Oakland University.

For the past ten years, they have been doing training programs throughout the United States on uprooting relations of domination, and alliance building, with a particular focus on issues of race and class. In this article, they point to the need for a renewed practice of community and describe some of the values in which it must be based.

If you suddenly became seriously ill and could no longer take care of your own needs, whom could you count on?

Whom would *you* rearrange your life for, if they got seriously ill? Would their needs be met by institutions?

If the banks suddenly collapsed and supermarkets closed, what would you do? Whom would you turn to? Who would turn to you?

If a natural disaster struck your area, do you assume government would step in and provide all the necessary relief?

Our answers reveal a great deal about our own sense of community. Prior to World War II, family and community ties were taken for granted in North American mainstream society. Community life meant caring for one another. When we became ill, we counted on neighbors, relatives, church members and friends for support and care. But in the generations following, communities gave way to urban and suburban sprawl, long distance families, and farflung networks of people, brought together by interest or work. Relationships were as easily lost as begun.

For a time, many people found the erosion of community bonds liberating. No longer constrained by nosy neighbors and provincial values, in the anonymity of big cities individuals felt free to develop and explore their identities. In suburbs, families were relieved of the weight of tradition and of dealing at close range with generational tensions. Many of the burdens of providing care for one another shifted from the shoulders of families to institutions. Elderly parents and grandparents were placed in "homes." The differently abled were put away. Natural disasters were handled by federal agencies. Insurance companies protected people from unexpected losses. Professionals of all sorts ministered to the needs of people.

"Competition is an acid corroding community ties, keeping society's dysfunctional relationships operative."

Today in North America we face a widening gap between rich and poor. Life for those at the bottom is becoming more and more harsh, and both middle and working class people are less and less secure as corporate power streamlines with mergers and layoffs. Now, with the dismantling of the welfare state, we can no longer count on the institutions that we have depended on in the past. Whatever their strengths and weaknesses, they have become luxuries. Few people believe government has either the will or the capability of providing any refuge. Institutions are increasingly helpless in the face of people's growing needs. Schools shut down for lack of money. Police avoid walking the streets of drug-infested neighborhoods. In the U.S., health insurance is outside the grasp of many working people. Public hospitals close their doors while ambulances shuffle the sick and wounded from one emergency room to another, hoping they will die en route. Roads crumble, bridges collapse, and every day brings a new environmental disaster while bureaucracies "study" the problems.

The word "freedom" strikes a deep chord in our psyche. For some, freedom has meant the opportunity to think, say or do what one chooses, to broaden one's options, to have no restraints. But freedom has unexpected costs. The underside of freedom is to have no social responsibilities. Some would argue that this is a good state of affairs, but their argument rings hollow as we reap the consequences of a culture devoid of a sense of responsibility to one another and to the Earth.

This "free country" mentality has created a culture of isolated individuals where image and access to material wealth are all that matter. The social consequences of people's actions are ignored by stressing good intentions, integrity is replaced by personality, and ethics are viewed as sentimental. Competition is an acid corroding community ties, keeping society's dysfunctional relationships operative.

A deep sense of alienation grips most Americans, leaving them in a void of isolation which they compulsively try to fill with television and commodities. As a result, violence has become a daily companion. The U.S. Senate Judiciary Committee recently released a report which acknowledged that the U.S. is the most violent and self-destructive nation on Earth. A record number of killings—at least 23,000—occurred in our country in 1990. This is a murder rate almost twice that of Northern Ireland, a country torn by civil war. For most of us, relations of brutality, force, humiliation and mistrust have become normal.

"Connection, caring, trust, enduring dependable relationships, generosity of spirit, and delight in difference—these are the values of healthy community."

Feeling empty on the inside, and separated from one another and the Earth, people long for community. This longing is especially acute in people with economic privilege, who are often several generations removed from true community life. For the sake of access to the ladder of upward mobility—in order to become urban, middle class, professional, cosmopolitan—ties to heritage, people and place, have been sacrificed. Conversely, it is among those *least* incorporated into the dominant society that, out of *necessity*, community survives.

In inner cities, small towns and rural areas, people are still in touch with caring and connected ways of living. It is no accident that those who grew up before World War II lead many of today's struggles resisting the most destructive aspects of late industrial capitalism. Elders—especially women—know from their own experience that life can be different. They are often in the forefront, from initiating efforts for protecting the sacred lands of Big Mountain, to reclaiming the streets from drug dealers in Detroit.

Connection, caring, trust, enduring dependable relationships, generosity of spirit, and delight in difference—these are the values of healthy community. To create the fundamental social changes that will enable us to live in harmony with each other and with the Earth, it is imperative to reclaim and restore community. We must develop relationships that enable us to celebrate the joys of daily life and survive its burdens with meaning, purpose and humor. As the state becomes increasingly violent and crude in its protection of power and privilege, community bonds form the basis for support and resistance.

Community is essential for meaningful collective action. In relations of trust, we experience the real freedom to explore different ideas and ways of being which are necessary to survive hardship and secure the future. When we *know* we can count on one another, conflicting views are no longer seen as threatening; instead they are welcomed because they broaden understanding. Only in community can we discover the best course of action, claim our power, and act in unity.

The conscious creation of community is not something we need to approach in a vacuum. The women's movement, and the gay, lesbian and bisexual liberation struggles have taught us much about how to build connections without recreating oppressive and dehumanizing elements. For example, "nosy neighbors" helped our children when they fell on the street, but they often turned a deaf ear to screams in the night as women suffered behind closed doors. Families' warmth and support became painful condemnation when their members claimed gay and lesbian identities.

"When we *know* we can count on one another, conflicting views are no longer seen as threatening; instead they are welcomed because they broaden understanding."

In the process of identifying and confronting these contradictions, the women's movement established principles for our relations: the notions that *all* perspectives have to be given voice, and that everyone's needs count. This provides a new basis for the development of a culture fostering connection without oppression, power without violence, and an appreciation of difference without abandoning principle. However imperfectly we move toward this vision, the quality of our relationships is at the center of what we do and how we are with one another.

Just as the concept of "the personal is political" has altered our collective understanding of political action, seeing community as the foundation of social action leads to fresh approaches in our work toward securing the future. Some people working for social change do not see community empowerment and community organizing as important; it lacks glitz. Often such work is slow, repetitive and small in its achievements: a window fixed here, a crackhouse closed there, a family given support, a dispute settled without guns—quiet changes. They do not lend themselves to prime time media coverage.

Such changes are often the work of women. "Women's work" has always been dismissed—the work of remembering the details, noticing the emotional nuances, keeping the peace, keeping food in the fridge and clothes laundered. Yet these seemingly mundane affairs form the basis of healthy community life. Women's ways weave the substance of community ties. We need to value these sensibilities and move them into public life.

"Without roots, movements, like trees, cannot survive the inevitable storms which their presence attracts. Community provides such roots."

Historically, these bonds have provided the energy, imagination, moral certainty and courage which have propelled movements of marginalized people. Women's resourcefulness has enabled movements to survive adversity. For example, in the labor struggles of the 1930s, women were not only organizers and strikers; their ingenuity enabled people to withstand months of strikes without pay. Deeply rooted in the immigrant and working-class communities surrounding the mills, mines, factories and packing plants, people encouraged one another to stand up to bosses and to sustain the belief that, in the end, they would prevail. Women also gave impetus to the civil rights movement; they crowded the halls of African-American churches and refused to ride the buses. Embedded in and growing out of the everyday lives of people, these movements raised fundamental questions.

Without roots, movements, like trees, cannot survive the inevitable storms which their presence attracts. Community provides such roots. The reclaiming of community is the only hope and promise for healing our society. This has great implications for both the content and the context of social change work. The following contrasting settings illustrate this.

The first example is one that many of us find all too familiar: an annual conference of a progressive, leftist organization. Most participants are white males from middle-class backgrounds. The air is filled with talk—abstract, intellectual, competitive, unemotional, analytical, earnest and never-ending; no laughter, music or celebration, but lots of literature. Decorating the room is one tired banner and plenty of abandoned half-filled styrofoam cups, with an occasional floating cigarette butt. Ironically, the purpose of the conference is to develop strategies to inspire folks.

In contrast are the Rainbow Quilters, who have decided to make quilts and sell them. They are Latina, African-American, European-American—mostly older women living on very little money. They get together to cut patterns, talk about the events of the day, share remedies for various aches and pains, take time for one another, and take care of business. They give earnings to a sister group in Nicaragua and to some of their members to help cover expenses to go on a delegation to El Salvador. At their yearly celebration, quilts of all colors and sizes brighten the room, each with a small tag listing the names of all those who worked on it. Ample food and drink are available, and lots of children are about. They unveil their new quilted sweatshirts, made for young people to convey the message of self-reliance.

In the United States, most of the resistance to the Persian Gulf War was male-defined: confronting the police and raising fists in the streets. In contrast, the women's organization *Madre* arranged a speaking tour entitled "Mother Courage." On a small stage in a packed auditorium in San Francisco, Alice Walker opened the evening with some of her poetry. Then the tour women came out. They were young and old, Jordanian, Palestinian, Israeli, and U.S. citizens of Iraqi descent. One by one, they told their stories: the nightmares of their children, harassment in the airport, fears for the safety of loved ones.

"The qualities embodied in our relationships over the kitchen table are the very qualities needed for our talk of strategies and actions."

Here, in the quiet voices of these women, were the strongest and most compelling reasons for peace, for resistance and for the need to find new ways of living together. At one point, a man in the audience made a snide remark to his companion about the Israeli speaker before she even began her talk, but soon he, too, was listening with a receptive ear. He could not maintain his oppositional stance in the intimate atmosphere the women created; there was nothing to feed the fires of dehumanization.

These contrasts reflect the emptiness of those struggling for change without community, and the hollowness of politics devoid of spiritual connection. Spirituality is that aspect of ourselves which enables us to transcend our isolation and move into communion with life and with one another. When our lives lack any kind of experience which connects us with the sanctity of life, it is as though we have lost the very ground of our being. Spirituality is central to community and to effective political work.

Let us welcome the changes that are taking place in political culture. Conference openings and closings with ceremony; meetings that include moments of silence; new rituals of play, celebration and grieving; candles that honor our dead, storytelling of our diverse heritages. When we trust our inner voice, we discover our visions of a better world, and deepen our connection to each other, to the Earth and to our convictions.

If we are to secure the future, we must reconstruct our communities. To do so, women's ways of talking, listening, and being together must come to define all public and political life. The qualities embodied in our relationships over the kitchen table are the very qualities needed for our talk of strategies and actions. If we do not consciously work to express these ways of being, we reproduce the alienating patterns of the dominant culture, even in progressive politics.

The familiar refrain—"To survive in a man's world, one must act like a man"—must be turned on its head. For the world to survive, *everyone* must act like a woman. Let us reweave our communities, reclaim the wholeness of life, and empower ourselves to heal the future.

6

Rediscovering Tribalism

An interview with Gawitrha' and Gowengani

As we ponder the potential of bioregional community for healing the Earth, we must inevitably look to the wisdom of aboriginal societies whose people have lived in communities in harmony with the land for countless centuries. In the following conversation, two people from the Six Nations Territory on the Grand River in Southern Ontario discuss the global crisis and their hopes for a revival of community in a framework of egalitarian tribal traditions.

Gawitrha' is an aboriginal North American by blood and by choice, a member of the Bear Clan of the Cayuga tribe of the Iroquois Confederacy. He has recently published a book-length essay, Dwanoha—One Earth, One Mind, One Path, on the themes touched on here. Gowengani is a Mohawk mother, soon to be a grandmother, and is a Faithkeeper in the Longhouse religion.

Gawitrha': In my younger years, my space was surrounded by walls of ignorance and apathy. The windows on those walls were not windows at all but merely pictures painted there for my "convenience" by those in power at that time. One of those images depicted people of colour working happily together under the direction of people wearing white hats. The window in another wall showed a beautiful landscape with healthy, luxuriant vegetation and contented animals. Yet another showed a church and a multitude of happy children surrounding a kindly priest. The final one was an awesome but reassuring image of a blindfolded goddess with a balance in one hand and a sword in the other.

According to my picture windows, all was right with the world and I could see no need for discontent. Until one day a friend invaded my space, rudely poked a hole through one of my beautiful picture windows, and challenged me to take a look out at the real world. As I approached the freshly made hole, I was surprised to hear sounds of great distress. Looking through, I saw huge mounds of bones and bodies of various colored people as far as the eye could see. Angry and confused, but curious, I rushed to the next window, and poked a hole through it myself. Sure enough, instead of lush vegetation and happy animals, I saw dead trees, fish floating belly up, and whole mountainsides clear-cut. And the same thing happened with each of the other windows when I poked through them. So that was my rude awakening to what was really going on out there.

Helen Forsey: *What do you see now as the fundamental causes for the mess that you saw through those windows—the mess that the planet's in now?*

Gawitrha': At first, I blamed everything on the white man. Finally I came to see that people—males—of all colors were wearing those white hats. That's when I realized the problem wasn't that simple. Wherever you look, the bad things that are happening on Earth always have an element of predation. I think that the evolved characteristics of the male hunter by necessity had to be predatory and vicious and even cruel. That spirit still walks this Earth in the form of males. Not all males, but it's still here, and it has been encouraged by the concepts contained in civilization, especially private property.

"Private property was the thing that opened Pandora's box and let those destructive male characteristics out to ravage the Earth."

Gowengani: I'd have to agree with that. It's pretty hard working with men, because it seems like their ego sort of gets ahead of them, and then they take over from there. Usually they talk a good word, but then you start watching their behavior, and it's sometimes opposite. I think the ego does a lot of damage there. And I also see that in women too, who have been working with men a lot, or who just try to become part of that hierarchy. That's not very healthy either.

HF: *How do you relate that behavior to the destruction of the Earth and all those other evils?*

Gawitrha': Within a tribal community, those male characteristics were kept in check because equality was an inherent part of tribalism. Private property cannot exist in tribal society. Private property creates social stratification and different levels of power. Private property was the thing that opened Pandora's box and let those destructive male characteristics out to ravage the Earth.

It doesn't really matter to the males how they get the power, whether they get it through cutting down ten thousand hectares of forest, or whatever. Whether it's in the form of a young woman alone, or a rainforest standing there that can't scream, it doesn't really matter. And it doesn't stop there. There just doesn't seem to be any limit to what they'll do if anything threatens their position.They don't use clubs and spears now, they use laws and computers. The principle's the same.

I suppose you could compare the problems on Earth to the symptoms of a disease. In fact, the behavior displayed by a virus is similar to that displayed by a "civilized" human male: it is intrusive, destructive, exploitive, manipulative and predatory. With a virus, there are certain conditions which activate this behavior, and others which discourage it. The same with a male. For example, there's the effect of private property, of drugs and alcohol, and of men in groups—those things seem to excite the predatory male tendencies.

"When people's economic and social interests overlap ... where they can depend on one another without any doubt, then they can establish this form of government and society."

HF: *So what directions should we be looking in for change, for healing?*

Gawitrha': Private property served to activate this virus, so I suppose our first step in the healing process would be to take a great big scalpel and cut the private property concept out of existence so that we'd have a better chance of existing again in an egalitarian manner. Egalitarianism guarantees human rights to freedom and dignity. There can be no equality or democracy in the present system. There's no healing to be had there. George Bush's "world order" is just more of the same.

Our prophecy talks about a change, so maybe we'll live to see that and maybe not. Our Longhouse religion talks about the coming faces, the children that are coming up. The realization of the coming faces has a stabilizing effect on us; it should, anyway.

HF: *What signs of hope do you see in your own community—things that will provide a basis for this kind of change?*

Gowengani: With the Confederacy, there are still the clans. I'm not saying that it operates totally as it used to. But it's still recognized. Now the kids are starting to look back at it and say, what is my clan, and who are my relatives, asking a lot of questions to the older ones. I believe it's starting to come back stronger. They're wanting to know their roots, and we have to get our heads together and start answering these questions.

Gawitrha': The clan system establishes your identity, but of course along with that, you have to commit yourself one hundred per cent. Your fellow clan people are your family, they're your people, and you live and die for them. That's what it's going to take, too, you know. That's how it was in the past. When people's economic and social interests overlap to that extent, where they can depend on one another without any doubt, then they can establish this form of government and society. Right away that eliminates the need for so many things. No more need, for example, for police, or prisons, or judges, because the people are working among themselves under a common interest. And then the alliances grow and spread. The Great Peace, when it was set down, that's what it did.

HF: *Do you see examples in communities outside of the native context, where people may be looking in the right directions but are hung up on some of the essential points?*

Gawitrha': We went down to the Farm in Tennessee fifteen years ago, for the sole purpose of talking to them and seeing if they would set themselves up in their own little micro-society according to a clan system, and try to establish some kind of a tribal association. I sort of zeroed in on the Farm because of its size; they had quite a few people down there. There was all that energy, and it could have been directed toward organizing under the clan system, because that goes a long ways, to have that together. But they wouldn't listen to me; Stephen Gaskin wouldn't even talk to me. The way it was there at that time, it seemed like he was the big Daddy and that's all there was to it.

The Basques in Spain have established these communities—they work quite well. The Mondragon co-operatives are world famous. They've found that in their cells, the most they can have to function is five hundred people. It's still not quite tribalism, but they function in a communal way, and their interests are overlapping. Although it's not completely egalitarian, they don't have a wide gap between the top level of income earners and the bottom.

Down here most of our people are lagging behind for several reasons. They're still into the American Dream; they don't see the culture slipping away from them.

Gowengani: I think it faded away due to the residential schools, how they pounded the culture out. I know for myself I have a lot of questions that I'm searching for right now, and I might never get the answer, but at least I'll be satisfied with trying.

Gawitrha': The school system here has intentionally kept the knowledge of our own culture away from us; that's been the policy ever since the Europeans landed. And you can understand why, because the system they found here was one in which private property couldn't survive. Their system is just the opposite; it can't stand to have a sharing kind of economy.

So that's been the policy all along; this is what necessarily took place in the schools. Our kids grew up not knowing a damn thing about their own identity, and that's why a lot of them are at sort of a dead end now. They go to the old-timers and they'll be told, no, that's not a good way, and yet everybody at the school is saying, Yeah, that's the way, you go for it. They end up with no direction, trying to find a direction of their own through different kinds of experimentations, not always wholesome.

"At a tribal level there's very little paperwork that you need."

HF: *It sounds as if you're kind of a bridging generation—people between thirty and sixty are in the middle, between the community's traditional ways and this new resurgence, which has all that youthful energy and curiosity but very little of the tradition?*

Gowengani: "Between" is the key word. I feel like I'm caught in between here, because my kids are asking me questions. I've got a grandchild on the way, and I'm thinking, wow, I've got a big job ahead of me, I've got to start finding these things out. But then you get out into the civilized world, and you're in between again. You're competing in that world, and in the other world you're supposed to be equal. It's pretty hard. I find that my forty-hour a week job gets in the way of my learning these things, of putting my total energy into that.

I'm glad that my daughter is learning the language. She's learning Cayuga; I'd say she's pretty fluent. But that's the language, and there needs to be more of the culture.

Gawitrha': It's good what they're doing, at least they're going in the right direction. Where Gowengani's going tonight is what they call a medicine type of a feast. They do that for people that have problems, all different kinds of problems. I guess you could say it's one of the things that have been kept. Even though we're surrounded by civilization, these things have been carried on. It would be hard to evaluate the total effect it's had on keeping people together over the years, keeping them well.

But there's a time factor here. We don't really have a lot of time left. It would be a damn shame to lose all that accumulated knowledge that people have gained over who knows how many thousands of years.

Gowengani: We have to turn to the elders or the ones who have been at the Longhouse that understand the language and ceremonies. A lot of times it's all symbolic, so you really have to think about how it affects your life, and what it means, some of the things that are done, what does it symbolize. Then it all turns toward thanksgiving, and the Earth, all the natural world. It's helpful.

Gawitrha': This mentality of thanksgiving that's contained in our teachings, it's something that the whole Earth could benefit from. It's far-reaching. It doesn't sound like much, but it's like a tree, it just branches. It's a mentality that has to be there in order for the healing process to take place, because it encompasses all living things, and there's no room for an unbalance like we see today. There's no room for all the things that have come from that, all the institutions, governments and whatever. All they are is a manifestation of the unbalance.

It's like this machine we had one time on the farm. We didn't really know how it worked, but we were trying to get it to run, and we'd adjust a little thing here, and then ten other things would be wrong. We just kept trying it, make a little adjustment here and there, and it would help one way, but then other things would go wrong. So it seems like that's the way this civilization is, they try this and try that, and it's just maddeningly complex. That's why you have these new high priests springing up, these new specialists in all these areas of expertise. They're dangerous too, the high priests. And there's no *need* for it to be that complicated. At a tribal level there's very little paperwork that you need.

I was at a conference about peace and freedom and so on, and I was asked, being the only native there, what I saw as the solution to the problems that we have on Earth. So that's what I suggested, you know—getting rid of private property and nation states. They asked me, really sneeringly, to please be more realistic, because, they said, private property and nation states are here to stay. And my answer to them was, that their very best scientists are trying to tell them that *human life* is not necessarily here to stay. So it's time for a radical change, there's no time for anything else.

"...the footprints are still visible, we can still follow them if we can find them. It takes a lot of commitment..."

HF: *So people who agree on that, what do we do now? Try to convince other people, and then act on it in our own communities?*

Gawitrha': That's about it. I guess it's just going to have to be through a process of awareness. Getting people to see how dangerous private property is. There's people out there that wouldn't want private property tampered with, so they've got to be persuaded that it is really a poison.

It might sound like a really off-the-wall thing to do, but maybe have someone bring it up in the United Nations, introduce a resolution to eliminate private property on a global scale. Once that idea's been put in somebody's mind, it seems to work on them. Just the idea causes a shift of consciousness. Because they'd never thought of it before. And then they toss it and turn it, and a lot of them might come up on our side.

HF: *I think especially in areas of the world that do not have as much material wealth as most of us do here. People here are scared to give up what we have for a sharing, egalitarian community.*

Gawitrha': This is why a spiritual basis for this kind of belief is important. If you believe in it, and especially if you grew up with it, then it becomes your second nature, you naturally share with everybody, and you expect everyone to reciprocate. But we're a long way from that yet.

If we went back 10,000 years, everybody was living that way. But there's still people practising it, the footprints are still visible, we can still follow them if we can find them. It takes a lot of commitment; I mean, life and death commitment. That's what it is anymore, it's a life and death game now.

Part Two
Difficulties, Dilemmas, and the Search for Balance

*I*f we gloss over the difficulties that people encounter in their communities, we cannot hope to build a better world. Sometimes in our enthusiasm we may give the impression that joining or creating an eco-village or a cooperative homestead is a relatively simple matter, and that once that is done, all our problems are solved. This is reminiscent of the old fairy tales with happy-ever-after endings.

Real life, in community as in other ecosystems, is rather different. Part Two focuses on some of the difficulties and dilemmas of community-building—particularly in the "crucible" that intentional communities provide—and reflects on what has been learned.

7

"The More We Do, The More We Know We Haven't Done"

An interview with Ira Wallace

Ira Wallace was a founder of Aloe Community in North Carolina, and later a member of Dandelion in Eastern Ontario before moving to Twin Oaks in Virginia in 1984. Gardener, child care worker, cook, networker and organizer extraordinaire, she has visited kibbutzim in Israel and numerous other communities in Europe, Mexico, Canada and the United States. She has been central to many of the most interesting and far-reaching initiatives both in her home communities and in the network organizations—the Federation of Egalitarian Communities and the Fellowship for Intentional Community—that she is involved with. With her dynamic energy, her warmth, humor and wisdom, and with the added perspective of her experience as a Black woman in a mainly white milieu, she has guided and reminded us, as she does in this interview, of the richness of difference, the complexity of connection, and the strength of commonality.

Helen Forsey: *Can you talk about bioregionalism, or environmental practices at Twin Oaks, and how important or unimportant they are there?*

Ira Wallace: Well, we did a long-range study, and as it turned out, growing our own food and trying to be energy self-sufficient was actually theoretically very high on people's priorities. But it's not the number one priority. For example, people aren't willing to change their eating habits to be in line with what we can grow here; or as a group to make major changes in our work scene to make sure we have more of our own food. Although we do produce a lot of our own food.

51

We do a lot of things; it's just bit by bit. We're researching having a hydro-electric plant on the old mill down on the river, making a deal with the owner about sharing the power. The tofu business, we thought maybe we might make some money, but we weren't sure. If it had been a less ecological business, there's no way we would have taken that risk. We've got the sewage treatment plant, the sawmill, all these solar installations. But I guess the more we do, the more we know we haven't done.

We have a whole long laundry list of things that we want to do and that we could afford to do, but no person wants to actually do the work that's necessary. For example, we have a bunch of older buildings that could use some serious work on insulation, but the less glamorous energy conservation things like that are going very slow, because nobody wants to do the work, cause it is *boring*.

Whereas it's true that when we do something new we try to do those things that we did not do or couldn't afford to do in the past. The new building, for example—that thing is tight as a drum, there ain't no leaks in that thing. It has solar heat and solar hot water, a wood furnace too, and it's wheelchair accessible. It's groovy.

HF: *There's a story to its name, isn't there? What's it called again?*

Ira Wallace: Nashoba. This was the name of some integrated commune right at the end of the Civil War. It was funny, we were thinking, "Oh, these people, they didn't do anything very groovy." No, they only risked their lives to do what they did. I mean just living together, Black and white people at that time was enough to be risking your life. But it didn't work out, and so we were saying, "Oh, too bad, they didn't really do anything." But you know, I wonder if I would do something, just for a principle, where somebody might kill me.

HF: *Can you tell me something about how you came to choose to live in intentional community yourself?*

Ira Wallace: Well, I grew up with grandparents. I lived in the city, and we had a garden which I had absolutely no interest in dealing with when I was a child. But then I went off to college, and you know, I just missed it! We were trying to partially work our way through school, and we were saving money for this homestead. It was around 1966, and we were reading stuff about "back to the land" and we thought we wanted to homestead after we got out of college. I don't know why we needed to get out of college to homestead, but that's literally how we thought about it! I was taking a class on utopian literature, and I got all excited about these intentional communities. So we went off to visit some, and came here to a Twin Oaks conference. We wanted to come and live at Twin Oaks then, but they wouldn't let us because we had a kid. And so we met some people and started Aloe instead of going off and having a homestead.

HF: *From your experience, do you think intentional communities like Twin Oaks are readily accessible to a variety of people from different racial or class backgrounds?*

Ira Wallace: You know, it's pleasant for me, the kind of country community that I'm in here at Twin Oaks, but I sometimes don't think that it is likely to give the benefits of cooperative living to people who are poor. Because of where it is, and because of the number of other things that we're experimenting with at the same time. Like, for example, how far along people are on issues around feminism. It's comfortable to live here at Twin Oaks around those issues, and yet it means that someone who has just been introduced to this, whose main goal in life has been trying to have enough money, and who hasn't ever really gone very far in school, would have problems. You know, they wouldn't understand the jokes in the hammock shop; something would always be being politically incorrect. I see our needing to have a high level of awareness about these things as being something that can keep some people who are Black or working-class from being able to live here. It's complicated.

"The kids here ... get more integrated into the work and the life of the community when they're more a part of their family and are doing things with mixed-age groups."

HF: *How do people in kibbutz deal with these kinds of issues, around differences?*

Ira Wallace: I think they have similar problems. Most of the people who live in kibbutzim are from Ashkenazic, Eastern European background. Over time, that's becoming less so, but a lot of that is because children who grew up in a kibbutz are going out and marrying people from different backgrounds, Sephardic people. About half of the kibbutz children come back, and a large number of them marry outsiders. It really changes the kibbutzim.

Sometimes they'll say, "Well, it's those people who don't want to come to us," but there are decisions that they've made that *make* people not want to! They've changed their minds on some of those decisions now, like the way they had the Children's Houses, with parents being really separate from children. Sephardic people, who are still in a more tribal situation, with the extended family and so forth, they just could not cope with that. Now for other reasons, kibbutzim have decided that it's better to have families be closer, and have the child-care program be more of an extended, better quality day-care or private schooling type of situation. Children don't sleep in Children's Houses hardly at all now.

HF: *How does that relate to Twin Oaks' experience with a Children's House? You've made similar changes, haven't you?*

Ira Wallace: Yes, and personally I have come to think that's a good thing. My experience around the kids here is that they get more integrated into the work and the life of the community when they're more a part of their family and are doing things with mixed-age groups, not just all kids their own age. On the kibbutzim they recognize that, and so they set up experiences for them to spend time working with people.

You know, maybe it doesn't make the kind of person we want, maybe it doesn't teach the kind of values of independence that we think we want, to require a person to be all the time with a pile of people their own age, doing things that somebody else decided they should be doing. There's an inconsistency there.

HF: *Are those issues around the children's program getting worked out, is that evolving more smoothly now at Twin Oaks?*

Ira Wallace: It's evolving, I don't know about more smoothly! It's just so funny to go places where they have more kids and they're more welcome, and the actual number of hours to take care of them is fewer than it is here for a very few kids, and kid behavior is better.

God, this kid stuff! You know how we really want things to be different from the way we grew up? And yet some of the things that were really the most valuable in our own growing up we throw out with the bathwater. Like just learning to work. I grew up without even questioning that every person did their share of the work, and started to do work at a very young age, not excessive amounts or anything. But that wasn't a high priority in what I wanted to teach my daughter; I wanted her to learn things I hadn't. And so she grew up picking up from people in community who feel like, "Oh, we work too much, work is so hard," and all this bullshit.

HF: *But wasn't there a lot of emphasis on work in the communities you were in, on integrating work and play, on work being a part of life and all that?*

Ira Wallace: I don't think that all this stuff we call work here, relates very much to actually supporting yourself. We only spend about a third of our work time at the kind of thing you could do to support yourself. And we're relatively inefficient about work. We tolerate extreme inefficiency, and flakiness, like changing your mind about responsibility. So we have a lot of emphasis on work, but we don't require good work behavior while we're doing it. And it's almost rude to talk about it.

On kibbutz, that was a different thing. There, they were into efficiency, and they rewarded it. If your work group got your work done early, maybe you could take off early, and maybe do something else. The natural reward of actually getting the stuff done right. Putting in your hours was not the major emphasis; getting the thing done was.

I'm certain with children you tell them that one of the ways that you're valued in society is that you contribute; everybody contributes something to the society according to what they can. And you expect something in relation to what the person can contribute, not just any old thing.

"You know how we really want things to be different from the way we grew up? And yet some of the things that were really the most valuable in our own growing up we throw out with the bathwater. Like just learning to work."

There's hardly any kid who's grown up out of Twin Oaks who's known how to do any mechanical stuff. And yet we have all the opportunity to teach them. Kids here tend to do the kind of work their own biological parents do. And the majority of people here do kind of white-collar work, or hammock-making. Even food processing and gardening are not considered fun. People see them as something you're going to *make* the kid do. It surprises me.

This is very different on kibbutz. There, manual work is very valued, and they sort of have an ideal of the worker-intellectual, so a really juicy person is one who can do farm work and stuff like that *and* talk about Plato or Jewish philosophers.

I mean, theoretically those things are valued here too, but how does that look when you only have a few people who have very many skills that way, and everybody else does something else, except for the odd time when they help with haying or something. It's like we're always fighting to have enough people to do auto repair, and garden, and stuff. Maybe that's North American middle-class culture. A lot of the people here who already know those things came from working-class backgrounds.

Now at Sandhill, for example, everyone who comes there has to share in doing farm chores. It's just like every person who comes to Twin Oaks has to learn how to make hammocks, even if they don't do very many. And because everyone has to do at least some farm chores at Sandhill, that's what you're changing toward when you go there. Whereas that's not the way it is here. If you happen to want to, you can do that kind of thing, and probably a third of the people actually take that option and learn something new—you know, woodworking or farm work or something. But it's not a part of the bottom line of what you do when you come here, what you try. And it doesn't have prestige.

HF: *What about political action? What is Twin Oaks' influence on the outside community?*

Ira Wallace: There are various things that have happened over the years. For example, there's a nuclear power plant not far from us, and eight or ten years ago they were going to store some kind of nuclear

---

Community Ethics—A Word of Warning

Janet Biehl

In most Westernized societies, community life has been eviscerated by the market, largely replaced by "an all-encompassing, wildly depersonalizing bureaucracy," as Murray Bookchin puts it. "The agency and the bureaucrat have become the substitutes for the family, the town and the neighborhood." In the face of the massive bureaucratization of life, most radical ecologists believe that we can build ecological societies at the community level, where people can meet and interact with each other on a face-to-face basis, care for each other, and know each other. Social ecologists have argued that the preservation and reconstruction of community life is necessary for an ecological society. Insofar as community life has been eviscerated in European and North American cultures, their ecology movements seek in various ways to preserve and restore community life as essential to the ethical fabric of human existence.

Indeed, it is here that the ecology and ecofeminist movements share aspirations with movements to oppose development in Third World countries. In non-Western cultures, many people seek to protect not only their natural environments but their very cultures and communities against the toxicity of Western development.

Community and the communitarian ethos have been controversial subjects of discussion in radical political thought in recent years. Some theorists have rightly pointed out, for example,

waste there. Well, about four people from Twin Oaks and about three people who live in the wider community made such a ruckus that it didn't happen. I mean, they thought that we had a huge organization! There were just seven people that went to the meetings, but they wrote articles, and then they got lots of other people to write letters, and we'd bring forty people to the public meetings. And as it turned out, actually, it got lots of people in the wider community interested, who actually are following all these hearings and stuff now much more than people at Twin Oaks. It also means that they have to have these public meetings

---

that life in many previous communitarian contexts has been notoriously oppressive to women. We cannot ignore the fact that male-oriented cosmologies have invoked "nature" pure and simple as a prescriptive ethical order for society, and disdainfully defined women by their biological role in reproduction. Clearly, any serious attempt to work with the concept of community must grapple with this patricentric tradition of women's "naturally" prescribed inferiority.

Moreover, the decentralized community, seen abstractly without due regard to democracy and confederalism, has the potential to become regressive in other ways as well. Homophobia, anti-Semitism, and other forms of racism, as well as sexism, may become part of a parochial communitarian ethos that does not confront the troubling history of "naturalistic" prescriptions of inferiority or perversion that are applied to certain groups of people. The communitarian ethos has a history of repressiveness and parochialism that cannot be ignored.

Given this history of community, then, it is necessary for the ecology movement to carefully rethink how it is going to construct community in a liberatory sense, so that such problems can be avoided. The new communities that we construct must not contain the hierarchical features, for example, of many of the communities that capitalism destroyed. It is necessary to understand what an enlightened community should be—one that preserves the closeness and intimacy and camaraderie of community life, yet that would not be so parochial as to permit Blacks once again to be excluded, or women to be raped or deprived of their reproductive freedom. The only way that community can be restored in a liberatory way is if people can make decisions about the life of the community as a whole.

and notify people in a way that is much more obvious than just this little notice on the back pages.

Another project involved a lot of houses in the county that didn't have indoor plumbing or adequate outhouses, that weren't really in a position to get plumbing. So we did this outhouse project, making outhouses, which actually led to some other people writing a grant to bring indoor plumbing to a lot of those houses later.

And right now we're doing this reading project, the Twin Oaks' Reading Group. We do tutoring in the school, and also here at Twin Oaks for the kids in the area, and we've started to get our first adult students. This one member here has this method that works really fast. There's a woman she's teaching, who'd been going to adult reading classes once a week for two years, and she'd basically only developed about a fifteen-word vocabulary, and she doubled that in two weeks of working with Piper. Now she's reading little books, and she has a small child, so she's practising on kids' books and then she reads them to her child. And so that's very exciting.

Then there's my preschool. We don't have many kids the same age here, so I've made it open to other kids in our local area. So that there's usually from two to four other kids that come. And we used to have the co-op school; that had a very good reputation. A lot of kids came there who'd had some problem with the public school, and it provided an alternative for them.

"One of the things that's interesting about the Fellowship for Intentional Community is that it's not necessarily defining community in the same way that we do here—it's a much broader, more inclusive thing."

HF: *What about political activism outside the community? Weren't some of you on walks for the homeless, against racism, against poverty?*

Ira Wallace: Well, we do these things. I don't know how much I believe in them. I think that for me it's a cyclical thing. It's like, "Such-and-such is a bad thing. I don't know that this march will help. But then again, I know if I don't do anything, that certainly won't help." So, lots of Twin Oaks' people go to demonstrations and marches, and volunteer for things, and help with workshops and conferences.

And we have a letter-writing brigade every month. We get stuff from Amnesty International and all kinds of other groups, and people bring all sorts of local political things, and certain people have their pet projects that they always bring stuff about. So there are lists of things to write about, and sample letters, and then you write to people. And what's really nice about a brigade is that, if you're not used to writing, you can look at somebody else's letter who's hot on that issue. And of course we give money away to assorted political causes and local things.

Sometimes I despair of ever making any progress. I used to think, if I just worked on it, we could have all these different races of people living here at Twin Oaks, and I don't really think that's likely to happen any more. But you know, one of the things that's interesting about the Fellowship for Intentional Community is that it's not necessarily defining community in the same way that we do here— it's a much broader, more inclusive thing. People don't have to be income-sharing, they don't have to be doing just what we're doing. With the Fellowship, I do think that I may be able to be working with groups that are really different from us, and being real allies with each other.

HF: *And sharing some of the wonderful things that Twin Oaks does have.*
Ira Wallace: Precisely.

8

Checking Ourselves Out: Power and Leadership in Community Work

The Four Worlds Exchange with Lori Marum, Doreen Sterling and Willy Wolf

The Four Worlds Exchange *is published by the Four Worlds Health Promotion Program, based in Pincher Creek, Alberta. It is a sister organization to the Four Worlds Development Project, a native-run program working out of the Faculty of Education of the University of Lethbridge. The* Exchange *provides a forum for native communities to share ideas and innovations, and to access information, resources, and technical assistance.*

This article is based on a panel discussion in which the Exchange *asked three experienced community development workers to comment on the problem of power in community work. The issues they raise are familiar ones, which apply not only to community development workers but also to all kinds of leadership in all types of community.*

Lori Marum worked in a variety of settings in rural Alaska for some twelve years, and is now an Assistant Professor of Social Work and Field Coordinator of Interior Campus Programs serving rural Alaska for the University of Fairbanks. Doreen Sterling, a Thompson Indian from Merrit, British Columbia, served as coordinator of the Spirit of the Rainbow Youth Program, and is now program coordinator for the Hey-way-noqu Healing Circle for Addictions, in Vancouver. Willy Wolf is a Lakota Indian from South Dakota who now works as a social researcher at the University of Colorado, Fort Collins, and as a community development consultant to native communities across the United States.

There is a battle going on in native communities. It's a battle against alcohol and drug abuse, against economic dependency and political oppression, against physical and sexual abuse, against poverty and ignorance, against racism and anger. It is a battle for dignity, independence, freedom, justice, health and happiness.

This battle is being fought in the hearts and minds of our people in native communities across Canada and the United States. At the front lines of this battle are people trying to help, trying to better the community and people around them. Front-line workers are the ones who implement the social and economic development programs designed to help native communities develop.

The men and women on the front lines struggle with some of the most complex problems known to humankind. How can a community overcome generations of oppression and abuse? How and why do people turn their lives around? What is culture and how does it affect our lives? How can we live in harmony with each other and our environment?

"When people trust you and your opinions, you have power that can be used for good or for selfish and negative purposes. When it is misused, it is very dangerous."

The heart and soul of community development is the work of empowering the people. Empowerment is the process of setting up situations so that other people have access to power: power to change things, power to heal themselves, power to build a better future.

Where does the power come from that flows all around and in and through a community development process? Ultimately, say native traditional elders, it comes from the Creator. From there it flows from within the hearts and minds of the people into whatever they think and do.

In the process of empowering people, the community development worker has power—power given to her by the community through their trust. When people trust you and your opinions, you have power that can be used for good or for selfish and negative purposes. When it is misused, it is very dangerous.

Four Worlds Exchange: *When you are at all successful in community work, people begin to look up to you. In a way, they give away some of their power to you. Have you experienced this?*

Lori Marum: It's so seductive, especially if you get into a position of power like I did. I got awards, recognition; I started thinking that I was hot stuff. People are starved for leaders, and many of us also crave recognition and power.

FWE: *It sounds like a perfect set-up for a dependent relationship. We need recognition; they need to look up to and depend on someone.*

Lori Marum: That's it. We get hooked into the old co-dependency thing. Our self-esteem is defined by forces outside of ourselves: by our public, our fans, our groupies and followers. We forget our spirituality. Oh, we continue to pay lip service to the idea that the Creator does it all, but deep down inside we've stopped believing it. We start to act and think that we're doing it. Boy, was I wrong. And did I ever crash.

Willy Wolf: For me there is always the danger that my ego will circumvent the process. I need to be very conscious of this when I am working in a community. I need to continue to focus on my own healing issues and spiritual development.

The barometer to measure my spirituality is the quality of humility I have. If I am working my own personal development plan, I will be able to maintain that balance; otherwise it's very hard.

Doreen Sterling: If you're working with people in the addictions field, they may look up to you as a kind of role model. Most people want to be well, and they are attracted to wellness. If you are someone who has sobered up, gone to treatment, maybe you have a job, maybe you can talk well, or maybe you take a little bit better care of yourself physically— then people will try to give away their power to you. Sometimes they do it sexually, sometimes politically.

"When you take on the role of "leader", you stop enlarging the circle."

No matter how it happens, if you allow yourself to fall into this trap, you are keeping the community sick; you are adding to the hurt and dependency. I've seen some real pied pipers. People gather around them, and sometimes they completely forget what they're supposed to be doing, and use the personal power that people give them against the community. Recovering communities don't need to be used any more than they already have. The abuse has to stop with us.

Lori Marum: When people transfer a great deal of faith and trust and responsibility to one person, it's very hard for that person to remain humble and connected to the real process.

FWE: *It's like a little switch clicks off in your head and you slide into the role of "leader" without even realizing it.*

Lori Marum: When you take on the role of "leader", you stop enlarging the circle. When that happens to community workers, we get caught up in the web of thinking mostly about who we are; some even start talking about their destiny! We forget who we are working for and what it's all about. The vision becomes clouded by personal interest and gain.

FWE: *And when that happens, we tend to talk about our "vision" instead of following it. We try to sell it to others as a way of covering up our desire for leadership.*

The Burwash Experience

Joan Newman Kuyek

A group of us in Sudbury, Ontario, who had been involved in a lengthy battle over jobs and housing with the various levels of government decided to form an organization called the Sudbury Citizens' Movement. Over the period of a year, we developed an idea for an abandoned prison farm thirty minutes' drive from the city on the Trans-Canada Highway.

The prison farm had over 26,000 acres of forest and grasslands. It was on a major canoe route and close to a provincial park of extraordinary beauty. Three thousand acres were cleared land, and in fact had once raised enough food to feed the entire prison population of 700 and a small village that was on the site. Fourteen years before, it had been self-sufficient in vegetables, meat and dairy production. The year before the provincial government closed it down in a construction boondoggle, they had put $4.5 million into renovations on the sixty-nine houses, thirty-eight-bed single staff quarters, six shops and three barns. There was also a gymnasium that had never been used, big enough for two basketball courts.

A feasibility study had been done on the site in 1975 by a large consulting firm, indicating that a number of business ideas were feasible, but would create only about eight to ten jobs each. Our group spent two entire years working out a plan for the site, and proposed that the Burwash prison farm was an ideal place for a

Doreen Sterling: We become the one person who has the answers, the ideas, or the information everybody needs. Or we think, unless you are into what I'm into, then you are not well. This way of acting makes the community sicker. It's not allowing people choices, when choices are exactly what people need to have.

FWE: *How can we avoid the power trap? Leadership isn't bad in itself, is it?*

Lori Marum: I don't think there is anyone that can't be affected by this problem of power. We need to stay group-centred. If you keep one person in the limelight, it's very likely that person's addictive patterns will be reactivated. It's a setup.

---

regenerative form of agriculture and an interlocking set of worker cooperatives engaged in farming, dairy processing, construction, tourism, and the establishment of a group home for kids who were presently in foster care. Our own study of the feasibility of this plan indicated it might be self-sufficient within ten years, but that it would require about $2 million investment from the Province in order to bring the housing, etc. back up to standard.

We spent two years building community support and pressuring the government to take us seriously. Finally, we had reached a level of community acceptance where the government was forced to take us seriously, and they responded by hiring a consulting firm to do a feasibility study. The study cost $80,000. In the end, they came to many of the same conclusions we had, but they said we were not feasible because we could only create thirty-five jobs in five years, and would not yet be self-sufficient.

There was no way in their conclusions for them to measure the impact of our proposal on the long-term health of the land or the forest. No way for them to measure the long-term benefits for the children that could be there instead of in a city foster home. No way for them to measure the benefits of restoring the housing instead of tearing it down. In fact their indices of "success" were such that the government could find it more feasible to sell the land to the Department of National Defense for sixty-five dollars an acre for a rifle range, and destroy the houses. They could only measure social benefits by the number of people we would have been able to take off the welfare roles. And because this enormous document from an expert said we were not feasible, we were unable to convince the press and the public.

Leaders are those who are working for the healing and development of the people. I think what needs to happen is that leaders need to check themselves out pretty regularly with other people. They need to ask other people how to re-centre themselves when they get off balance, how to tell when they're off base, how to humble themselves. *Talk* to people about how you are feeling inside, about the recognition you are getting, about the seductiveness of power. And question yourself—always question your role. What are you really doing? What are you offering the people? Is this offering appropriate or oppressive?

Willy Wolf: One of the areas I notice community development workers struggling with is the issue of human sexuality. There is no quicker way to destroy the level of trust and intimacy you have established in the community than to get involved in sexual misconduct. We see sexual acting-out taking many forms, and it is very serious.

"There is no quicker way to destroy the level of trust and intimacy you have established in the community than to get involved in sexual misconduct."

When we create an environment such as a talking circle where we make it okay for people to share, to open up about anything that is affecting their lives, people feel incredibly vulnerable. If you are not in a good space, if you are not centred, you may find yourself pulled in by someone who is very vulnerable. A lot of people are looking for someone to fix them. You are there to help people past dependency, not to feed it.

Doreen Sterling: If you know you have power and control over people in a community situation, you can use it to help to free them, or you can abuse it. You can become a carrier of disease. Who of us wants to do that?

9

Of Mice and Elephants: The Individual, Community and Society

Paige Cousineau

The theme of the individual in community and society is a recurring one, and takes on a particular acuteness in intentional communities. In this article, Paige Cousineau reflects on her decade and an half with one such community, which she finally left in 1983. "The main motivating force behind my life choices to date," she says, "has been the search for a social environment that permits and supports my freedom and power to create my own responsible destiny in the world. Now that's a mouthful, but what it has turned out to mean in practice is doing social change." Paige now lives and works in Hull, Quebec.

One day in my third year of university, I woke up realizing that the university wasn't *me* and I wanted to participate in real life. After brief and unsatisfying stints with no answers at Haight Ashbury, Rochdale College, and the Company of Young Canadians, I encountered a group working in a Black ghetto in Chicago in the '60s. A white group, called the Ecumenical Institute.

Now, *this* group knew what *it* was doing. It was out to renew the church, starting with the grass roots—the local congregation and its parish. The key mechanism was an intensive 44-hour weekend course on the fundamentals of Christianity—in its modern, post-World War II, existential incarnation. In the beginning, the Institute had a thoroughgoing base of intellectual ferment, because most of the full-time members were ex-university staff, or clergy, or at least university graduates. Added to this was a conviction that a church person was supposed to be "on the revolutionary edge of history."

The community was tightly knit, and *very* missional; hence, highly structured. Che Guevara was the heroic image the fall I first joined, and common study was Franz Fanon's *Wretched of the Earth*. My first four years in the community were a real city-of-the-universe education. The intellectual, social and group methods I learned there have been extremely powerful tools for me all my adult life.

In 1967 when I joined, the Institute consisted of some 150 adults and perhaps fifty or sixty children, almost all Americans; my partner and I were among its first international members. We lived in a seminary taken over from the Bethany Brethren who had left the neighbourhood when it turned Black. There were also three or four nearby apartment buildings which housed members. Small apartments were allocated to family units on the basis of one room per adult, and one half room per child. Meals were served communally, with the children eating together in a separate space. Each adult had a monthly stipend to cover personal expenses beyond food and shelter, with an additional allowance for each child.

"Intentional communities have an identity crisis or shift in four- to six-year cycles. To survive longer than one cycle, the community must recreate itself and redefine its purpose and identity."

In those days, about half of us had regular jobs—teachers, nurses, social workers, office staff—and from our pooled earnings we paid for all the community's expenses. The other half of the adults "worked in," maintaining the Institute's facilities, or running the neighborhood preschool, the health-care clinic, the adult self-help groups, the housing rehabilitation projects, or the print shop. These folks also organized the logistics of our weekend courses and of our own community life. We were a white island in Black Chicago's West-side ghetto. All of the neighborhood programs had come into being as a result of over six years of work with the Black community in the sixteen-block area around the seminary, called "Fifth City."

From five to six a.m. every day, all the adults except the breakfast team would gather for an hour of exciting intellectual activity-discussions, reports, planning, study, followed by a half-hour of Christian ritual. Two nights a week were devoted to book studies, one secular and one religious, and Monday night was "Family Night." Sunday afternoons were free time—I often slept.

Eight weekends out of thirteen we spent teaching one of the Institute's Friday-to-Sunday courses, in Chicago or in some church basement somewhere else in the U.S. or Canada. I remember teaching "The Twentieth Century Theological Revolution" in Omaha, Nebraska, and "The City and the Polis" in Lexington, Kentucky. What an adventure it was for a little Canuck straight out of school!

The last five weekends of each quarter, we spent evaluating, planning, and celebrating. An eight-week summer program each year in Chicago culminated in an Institute-wide planning and celebration Council. I remember one time we persuaded the poshest hotel on State Street to donate rooms for the entire community for the weekend; we were shuttled from the transit stop the six blocks to the hotel in three big black limousines!

But it was changing. It seems to me that intentional communities have an identity crisis or shift in four- to six-year cycles. To survive longer than one cycle, the community must recreate itself and redefine its purpose and identity. Many groups don't recognize this, and the more devoted the community is to its defined mission, the more likely it is to flunk the transition.

From about 1970, the Institute began to establish Regional Houses, consisting of six or more adults and their children, in different parts of the U.S. At the same time, we began our first community project outside the U.S., with Aboriginals in Australia. I think we negotiated that shift fairly self-consciously, and our numbers exploded—from 300 to 2,000 in about four years.

The next shift we did not catch self-consciously. An intentional community can never afford to forget that it is, for all its utopian visions, still a part of a national and world society. The economic prosperity of the sixties had allowed us in the Institute to change our outside jobs every year according to where we needed people's energy, and still be totally self-supporting with only half our members in paid jobs. We failed to recognize the global economic shift from the time of plenty in the sixties to the recessionary-inflationary period that began with the 1972 oil crisis. The members of the community—in the image of spiritual poverty—became actually poor; yet we continued to move people from place to place every year regardless of the hardship it imposed on them and on our life as a community.

Culturally, the revolutionary edge was now women's liberation, with the Equal Rights Amendment (ERA) in the States and the Women's Decade internationally. Funny how a Christian, clergy-dominated organization missed that one! I am sad to say that as a community we lifted not a finger to push Illinois to ratify the ERA. The party line was: "The women's revolution is done in our outfit; let's get on to the real action—community development."

"The well-spring of community relevance to the individual, and hence of community growth, is awareness of, and dialogue with, the changing natural and social environment."

By 1976 I was in total rebellion. I had started sneaking out of the group structures to go to National Organization for Women meetings, and the cloud of anger around me was visible to all but myself. I had mastered most of the Institute's curriculum, was an accomplished group leader, had work experience as a computer programmer and associate engineer, and had been to India and Europe as well as much of the U.S. I was now able to see some of the flaws in the community and even to question intellectually some of its ideas, particularly on gender roles. But I, and those who felt similarly, had no audience within the Institute.

Recognizing the breaking up of old forms, discerning what must be made new from what must be preserved, is an extremely hazardous period of trial for a community. Parallel to this, and part of it, are the journeys of the individual members. The well-spring of community relevance to the individual, and hence of community growth, is awareness of, and dialogue with, the changing natural and social environment. This dialogue takes place through, and because of, individual members' explorations outside of the group. To be free, the community must recognize and support the individual's journey, without exerting undue pressure to identify exclusively with the group.

The relationship between the individual and society is a symbiosis. Society needs my energy and I need its sufferance and support. But I am the mouse, society the elephant, and it may never notice my suffering or even death when it rolls over.

Now, is the smaller elephant, the intentional community, really any different? As a mouse, am I better off with a smaller elephant whose ear I can get closer to, but which must still function within the herd of full-sized elephants? Do I have more leverage on the herd's direction by having proportionately more influence on the wee one's direction? Or am I simply adding to the number of levels of obligation between me and self-fulfilment?

The answer may lie in the way the community defines its goal. A very precise goal or mission might seem to amplify my power for social change insofar as my personal goals match those of the group. However, I may be handing over my individual purpose to the community once I join it.

This tendency of the larger body to subsume—or occasionally consume—a smaller one seems to be a universal law, rather akin to gravity. The trick is for the mouse and the elephant to achieve a structural balance that recognizes and supports both of them.

As an employed member of mainstream Canadian society, I now have more privacy and personal space and am better off materially than I was in intentional community. But our society separates individuals from each other to such a degree that the result is atomization and alienation. Today I am very aware of the social forces upon me that militate towards wage-slavery because of my individual vulnerability. Like the medieval serfs who had to work several days each month for the lord of the manor, as a taxpayer I now work several months of the year exclusively for the government.

In the community to which I belonged for so long, this dynamic played itself out in the other direction. Because we, as individuals, identified so completely with the goals of the community, there was a constant tendency to dissolve the boundary between individual and group time—in favor of accomplishing group tasks. Over time, this resulted in burn-out and unexpressed feelings of resentment of the community by the members. It also showed up in community decisions made about how much energy and money to divert from the mission and direct towards living conditions of individual members (such as stipends, food, medical, dental and old age insurances).

"An acid indicator of the community's responsiveness to change is its attitude to ex-members. Are they a positive resource, or are they outcasts? And do the ex-members feel the same way?"

The more a community's culture supports individual destiny and creativity, the more likely it is to be able to hold a healthy tension between its collective mission and personal freedom, and therefore, the more likely it is to actually enable the individual's work for social change.

Joining a community is a response to a particular phase in a person's life experience. When that phase ends, the person is forced, either willingly or painfully, to re-examine the usefulness of the community in achieving her goals.

The risk, from the community's perspective, is losing members. Failure to take this risk, however, sets community goals above the individual's needs, and forces leaving the group to become a shameful rupture rather than a natural process of ebb and flow. In fact, an acid indicator of the community's responsiveness to change is its attitude to ex-members. Are they a positive resource, or are they outcasts? And do the ex-members feel the same way?

"An intentional community provides a space and a social structure for fresh visions to be tested and refined against reality, as well as for the testing and refining of individuals themselves."

Paradoxically (isn't life always paradoxical?), concerned but supportive caring about a person's decision to leave allows for the possibility of return, and actually contributes to long-term community survival. The group's struggle to identify the meaning of the departure in its own life will contribute significantly to its ability to recognize and successfully negotiate its own identity crises.

It is clear to me that change is only accomplished by communities of like-minded individuals. Moreover, if the individual member of society is not affected, there has been no real social change. In order for a significant shift to occur, pioneering experiments must be created to demonstrate ways in which social structures can incorporate the new idea. An intentional community provides a space and a social structure for fresh visions to be tested and refined against reality, as well as for the testing and refining of individuals themselves.

So it is not surprising that any era of major cultural change witnesses an upsurge in the formation of alternative communities. Socially, these communities hatch new responses to the breaking up of old forms. And it is from their individual members' experiences that communities get their feedback and inspiration for transformation, contributing in turn to the transformation of society as a whole.

The Death of the Small Commune
Marge Piercy

The death of the small commune
is almost accomplished.
I find it hard now to believe
in connection beyond the couple,
hard as broken bone.
Time for withdrawing and healing.
Time for lonely work
spun out of the torn gut.
Time for touching turned up earth,
for trickling seed from the palm,
thinning the shoots of green herb.
What we wanted to build
was a way station for journeying
to a new world,
but we could not agree long enough
to build the second wall,
could not love long enough
to move the heavy stone on stone,
not listen with patience
to make a good plan,
we could not agree.
Nothing remains but a shallow hole,
nothing remains
but a hole
in everything.

10

Community as Crucible

A conversation with Laird Sandhill

Those who know Laird Sandhill as communitarian, facilitator, and friend, find in him a wealth of stimulating ideas and compassionate insights into the joys, dilemmas and contradictions of the intentional community experience. In the following dialogue, he addresses some of these issues and shares some of his own experiences and hopes.

Helen Forsey: *The community I live in now used to be a lot more collective and close-knit fifteen or twenty years ago, but people found they had to have more distance in order to get along better with each other. They started doing less together, and now the group is very stable and friendly and mutually supportive, but loose-knit. There's a lot more distance and independence, a kind of balance they found was necessary for them.*

Laird Sandhill: That's a good point to try to address. One of the things I would raise as a countering question is that in any situation, the different aspects of everyday living which tend to be particularly onerous have to be dealt with by *someone*. I think that if you're not relying on a community setting with some kind of central economy or shared resources, then you are likely plugging into another system that has hidden exploitation. That is, somebody's doing that onerous work someplace; it's just out of sight.

In our community what we're trying to do is face the consequences of our choices, and not keep them hidden. We want actually to deal with the issue of that oppression here at home. Doing things as a group usually means that less of that onerous stuff is going to fall to any one individual than it would if we were fragmented on our own.

For example, everyone takes a turn cooking and cleaning, in rotation. Each person is required to spend only a small fraction of their time on this work, and no one is exploiting anyone else. We also try to rely on technology that we can maintain ourselves, keeping the issues around production and consumption more directly in front of us. We do not, for example, own a computer, partly because we don't know how to maintain the equipment, and partly because of the toxicity of silicon chip manufacture.

"One of the hardest but yet one of the most exciting things to me about communities is the process work we do around egalitarian, non-hierarchical decision-making."

One of the things you often find in groups that are less communal is more vehicles per person, or fewer people per building, that kind of thing. Who's pumping the gasoline? Where is the energy coming from? That analysis just trips right on down the road. Because most of us in community tend to come from more privileged backgrounds, we're better able to make the system work for us, dysfunctional though it is. And those kinds of exploitation are just a little more hidden.

But I don't want to come down too heavily on it, because the deeper you get into it, the more you feel, "Oh, my god, there's no end!" It's uncomfortable to do that analysis. You're constantly short of the ideal, and there's still more analysis to do. It gets almost to the point where it's hard to sit back and laugh, or take time off, because somebody's still out there suffering while you're taking a break. But you can't run your spirit down like that. It's just part of the balance question—something we're learning, something there aren't really good models for yet.

One of the hardest but yet one of the most exciting things to me about communities is the process work we do around egalitarian, non-hierarchical decision-making. It doesn't mean everyone's got to do the same things or everyone has exactly the same power, but you certainly strive for equal access and opportunity for input, and honoring what everyone can bring to the group. That work is at the same time one of the most exciting things and one of the most exasperating and draining aspects of community.

HF: *A lot of people who've previously lived in very close-knit communities have found that that degree of intensity, of integration with everybody else, was not sustainable for them, that they needed to get away from it. Not in order to fragment their lives or their commitment, but to have a space where they weren't actively doing everything so closely with other people all the time.*

Laird Sandhill: I'm clear that the intensive process work that's necessary in our communities is one of the things that many people are glad to be rid of. A lot of times, the progress in understanding it and seeing the power of it is so slow compared with the costs, that people just can't get away from it fast enough. And they're perfectly willing, after years of honest trying, to go ahead and engage in more housework, more commuting, more of all these generally unpleasant things, in exchange for not having to go to meetings! I think that's part of the price we pay as pioneers. Some people have been very courageous to make a big leap, and it's been an enormous struggle for a lot of people. We're out there groping in the dark and our learning curve has got a real slow ascent in a lot of cases.

HF: *If it's so difficult, why bother? What are the rewards of that kind of intensity, that unrelenting hard emotional and intellectual work?*

Laird Sandhill: I know of no better environment than community for making progress on knowing yourself and knowing others and how things work. We engage in political issues through actually trying to create something—not just talking about it, but offering models of how things could be different. We're trying to bring these issues into every aspect of our lives and to weave a whole from it all. It's very exciting and very challenging, and it leads to a tremendous sense of aliveness—there's nothing dull about it!

"I know of no better environment than community for making progress on knowing yourself and knowing others and how things work."

It's like a crucible: the heat of it, the intensity. Community allows for a greater concentration of breakthroughs, and faster progress, surer progress. And yet it can also be dangerous; the hurt can be greater, the sense of being overwhelmed or betrayed. There can be this real wild swing, from joyous "Ah-hah" moments to almost depression.

HF: *It can also be sheer hell. There are dynamics that can happen, and precisely because it's all so intense and you can't easily get away from it, it can be as bad as anything that happens in families, and that's saying a mouthful.*

Laird Sandhill: Yes, it can be destructive; it's possible to have abuses. People can get into things that they're not capable of finding a healthy way out of. Sometimes people aren't really in alignment any more but they're acting as if they are, and then abuses occur. It's important work to check those things from time to time. In cases where it gets nasty, especially where people are engaging in practices that they don't know how to control, there's no place to get away to sometimes, and it can be very difficult.

Part of what I'm talking about is the need for a group to do their work of being clear about what their common bonds are, making sure that the opportunities are always there for people to grow and move. We have to move forward only on the basis of drawing in everybody's contribution. It's hard work to do that, and it's an ideal we often fall short of. It's part of our struggling as a movement, even as a culture.

"As a traditionally raised male, it has been especially difficult work for me to learn to open up to emotional input—both mine and others'."

HF: *So this work that some of you have been researching and developing in the crucible of our communities—this group facilitation, consensus process, and mediation work—all that is an essential part of creating workable models for social change?*

Laird Sandhill: Absolutely. In particular, the aspect of how to work, not just with the ideas and the architecture of meetings, but also with the emotive input that people bring to them. You must work with all of it. I can recall many moments when different lightbulbs have clicked on in my head, but probably no realization has been more illuminating than the power and necessity of embracing people's feelings when doing group work. As a traditionally raised male, it has been especially difficult work for me to learn to open up to emotional input—both mine and others'. Yet, having engaged in that now, I find it to be among the most potent avenues for personal growth and for developing my skills as a group facilitator.

I wonder how much people have even had the experience of good meetings. I run into people at some of these networking meetings who say, "I can't believe the meeting went like that! It was so pleasant, so productive!" To me that's normal now, but for some of these people it's like, "I always dreamed it could be this way but I've never seen it before!" It's great fun watching their lightbulbs pop on.

I think that community has the ability to contribute to the society way out of proportion to our numbers, because the experience of things like that tends to be universal in value. Having gone through the crucible, we're tempered, and able to contribute more.

HF: *What do you think the future holds for intentional communities?*

Laird Sandhill: One of the challenges that's up ahead of us now is going to be the demographic transition—how will we work with the upcoming generations. When we get through this pioneering stage, what are our children going to do? You look at places like Twin Oaks and East Wind, and their history has been that very few kids actually go through all of their growing up there. They spend a few years, and then there are issues around integrating parents and non-parents, and it's still a struggle; we're not done with that.

HF: *In spite of the fact that it sometimes feels like one of our failures that kids don't stay, there is still that very important formative year or so in community. That time can be pretty amazing for a kid, a total change from what they've had before, and that's going to be there for the rest of their lives.*

Laird Sandhill: Yes, the impact can be there—the influence, even if the exposure is brief, relative to a person's whole childhood. What that will actually add up to in terms of contributions, impact on the society, who knows yet? And we do have kids now that have been in community all their lives. You know, my childhood wasn't like theirs; and I mean in very dramatic ways! So I look at these kids and I think, what is this going to be like, what are they going to do with this?

"We do have kids now that have been in community all their lives ... I look at these kids and I think, what is this going to be like, what are they going to do with this?"

One of the encouraging signs for me, that makes me think some corner is being turned, is that unlike ourselves ten or fifteen years ago, new groups now seem more ready to ask for help, early. They don't feel like, "By god, we have to do this on our own," which is really an extrapolation of the rugged individualism bullshit that we've bought into in our culture. Some of us had gotten out of it far enough to try group living, but not far enough to think, "We don't have to make this all up on our own. We can talk openly about our struggles, ask for help, and learn quicker." That's something my community wasn't smart enough to do back when we started. In our supreme naiveté, the four of us didn't even think about joining an existing community. We were sure that the way to get what you wanted was to start your own and create it in your image, you know, just like God did. And oh, my lord, we knew so little about what we were doing! Looking back on it, I just can't imagine how we survived. There was no end to what we didn't know.

I see a lot of young groups now advancing much faster because they don't fall into that trap of arrogance. It may be that there's just generally better awareness that there are resources out there. I mean, we didn't know where to turn to years ago. And now maybe people start to know. So that's exciting. I'm very encouraged about the prospects for community in this coming decade.

Drawing by
Maureen Swann

Part Three
From Vision to Reality: The Current Evolutionary Challenge

*I*f indeed it is true that bioregional communities will be the key to any
healthy future for life on Earth, how do we get from here to there? The
examples in Part Three show how a wide range of community efforts are
creating new realities in the midst of the old—circles of strength whose
influence is already rippling outwards to touch more and more people and
places with healing.

11

Sowing the Seeds of Change: An Urban Experience

Lucie Lavoie

If we are not to find the city an alienating and even deadening environment, those who live there must take on the responsibility of reclaiming it and shaping it anew according to principles of bioregionalism and community. As we see in the following account, this kind of communitybuilding happens through the cumulative effect of a multitude of small actions, each one of which is important.

Lucie Lavoie is a renegade forester, activist and wordsmith whose love of the forest led her to spend several months in India in 1990 working with the brave tree-hugging women of the Chipko movement. She chairs the Forest Caucus of the Ontario Environment Network, co-founded Friends of the Forest in Thunder Bay, Ontario, and teaches environmental studies at Confederation College there. She has made the conscious choice to build community, not out in the wilderness, but in the built environment of the Northwestern Ontario city on the shores of Lake Superior where she makes her home.

City life can be an alienating experience because there is little to nourish the spirit in an urban environment. I have often yearned for the wildness of the forest while doing battle with cars and trucks to keep my bicycle on an icy autumn road, or while watching my neighbors cut trees and pave former gardens. At such times I remind myself that almost half the people on this planet now live in cities, and it is in this urban setting that life-affirming communities *must* take root if we are to survive. There is much work to do.

Like many people who believe that change begins at home, my partner and I have spent the past decade building a life which minimizes collaboration with the present economic system. We do not wish to

81

support a structure which places economic gain above ecological integrity or human dignity. We object to the hierarchical, male-dominated, competitive nature of the present system, and know that co-operation and consensual decision-making are more equitable and affirming processes around which to organize. We also feel that a decentralized approach to decision-making enables communities to have a greater voice in making meaningful choices on issues like resource use and distribution of wealth. Our lives are therefore an act of resistance, a refusal to co-operate with the present economic system, by meeting our needs as far as possible from outside the mainstream economy and from within our own bioregion.

"The urban community to which I belong is not bounded by physical space. It does not exist within the confines of a neighborhood or a section of the city."

However, there is little comfort in striving to live sustainably as individuals and family groups when the planet's life-support systems are being destroyed around us. To be effective, our efforts must ripple into the lives of our urban neighbors. Those of us who work towards self-sufficient lifestyles are therefore beginning to work collectively, with shared vision, to build compassionate, self-reliant and equitable communities.

The urban community to which I belong is not bounded by physical space. It does not exist within the confines of a neighborhood or a section of the city. Rather, our community exists in the relationships which we build with each other all across the cityscape. Our community is one of shared perspectives and aspirations; it is built on true democratic processes, on processes where people are accountable to each other and to the planet, on processes which restore human dignity and improve quality of life. It is my belief that co-operative, supportive, empowering communities like these shine like beacons to attract fugitives from the exploitation and domination of the present economic system.

The people at the center of our urban community are connected in a meaningful way to each other as individuals and to the physical world in which we live. Each one of us is, in one way or other, an activist because we have been sowing seeds of change in the city. We have been working to create an equitable, peaceful, self-reliant society.

The women at the Women's Center, for instance, are part of my community. They provide support for women, whether they be survivors of family violence, incest survivors, or simply survivors of modern life. In addition to support, the Center provides information which puts the difficulties of women into a larger political context, and increases their access to decision-makers. The Center is also a place to organize and to share information. It is a place to give child care, to find a roommate, to stuff newsletters, or to have a cup of tea. These things are all important.

"We initially recognized each other by our attempts as individuals to create social change; now, some of us are beginning to engage in more deliberate forms of community-building."

The people who share my love of the woods are also at the center of my urban community. We spend many hours together each month, searching for the means to stop the destruction of global forests. We wonder how to inspire others to respect trees: perhaps we should organize more community treeplants and public lectures? Then we get mired in the complexities of multinational forestry corporations, trying to trace the faces of those that wield the power. We ponder the mysteries of spruce swamps, and what appear to be the even greater intricacies of bookkeeping and fundraising, while eating the cookies left over from our last event. These things are all important.

There are those people in my community with whom I spent many weekends sorting filthy beverage and food cans for recycling. There are those people who brought cans to the depot for sorting, then stayed to help, in spite of weather cold enough to freeze our eyelashes. There are those who come on clandestine nighttime raids with me to plant trees along city boulevards, those who bring their compost to our house because they live in an apartment and can't find any worms, and those with whom I dance my love for life. There are those who bring us scrap lumber which we recycle in our ongoing house-renovation projects, those who risked their freedom with me at a blockade for a river, those with whom I swap gardening tips and seeds, and those who massage my body when my heart is sick with despair. There are so many faces in our urban community, every one of us teaching and every one of us learning.

We have come together as a community because we believe that institutions must change profoundly if we are to survive on this planet. The present system which exploits and disenfranchises people, reducing humans and the planet to economic resources, must be changed. We initially recognized each other by our attempts as individuals to create social change; now, some of us are beginning to engage in more deliberate forms of community-building. We are working together to build alternatives to the present system.

Meaningful urban communities must make use of small local economies; local economies restore power to the people by bringing decision-making closer to home. For instance, a small local economy has arisen around food production in our city. Some of us engage in and promote urban organic farming, and belong to a food co-operative which orders bulk shipments of dry goods which we cannot grow locally. We promote, and sometimes contribute to, the local farmers' market, and are working on establishing community gardens for apartment dwellers. To support local businesses, we purchase other food and grocery items at small family-owned stores. These activities all help to place control over the production and distribution of food into local hands.

"We hope that restoring the spiritual link between humanity and the living planet will enable people to recognize materialism as a hollow shell which provides little satisfaction."

Another aspect of developing local economies is participation in an informal barter and exchange network, where skills, labor or surplus are traded. Since many of us are considered poor by current economic standards, bartering is a return to wise and equitable trading relations.

Many people in our community recognize the need to heal the cityscape. We must peel back the layers of concrete under which life is buried; we must challenge traditional urban landscaping tenets which often espouse nothing more than control over all aspects of nature. There is much work to be done: rejuvenating plant and animal life around the remains of streambeds, allowing nature to reclaim vacant lots, and restoring urban forests, will help to reconnect people to the Earth. We hope that restoring the spiritual link between humanity and the living planet will enable people to recognize materialism as a hollow shell which provides little satisfaction.

There are doubtless many other structures and values which our community should embrace, but we do not move quickly. We are taking the time to grow strong roots which will anchor us to the Earth through the turbulent times that are ahead.

As I go about my daily life, I keep a vision of the cityscape which I want to inhabit firmly planted in my mind; this vision guides my actions.

Houses nestle under the broad canopy of the boreal forest which is home to chickadees, chipmunks and red squirrels. Television sets sit idle during the four crucial months of growing season while their owners produce food in backyards, vacant lots or on balconies. Vacant industrial areas are overrun with wildflowers and young forests. The urban infrastructure supports renewable energy options: even in this bioregion characterized by wonderfully frozen winters, homes are no longer attached to the power grid but are heated and powered by sun and wind. Grey water and human faeces are composted and recycled, reducing the burden on our sewage treatment facilities. My bicycle and I travel unimpeded on a road built just for us. One day each week, my neighbors join together in labor for the good of the community.

In my utopian vision of the city, people live with fewer material goods but with a wealth of support and hope. This vision is my challenge. As I work to create meaningful urban community, I draw sustenance and encouragement from the earth I till, the trees which increase in girth in my front yard, and the people who work at my side.

12

A Passion for Women's World

An interview with Sonia Johnson and Jean Tait

Sonia Johnson and Jean Tait are founding members of a women's intentional community called Wildfire in the mountains of New Mexico. Sonia is best known as an inspiring speaker and author who was excommunicated from the Mormon church in 1979 for her support of the Equal Rights Amendment to the U.S. constitution. Jean has been an herbalist and alternative health worker. Both women are passionately committed to exploring and creating a new world beyond patriarchy. In this interview, they discuss what they have learned about what does and doesn't work.

Helen Forsey: *There's a lot of interest in intentional community among people who are serious about making a new world. What would you say are the basic preconditions for building a community that works?*

Sonia Johnson: Whatever you care about, you need to find other people who care about that. The comunity you live with needs to have its first priorities pretty much the same. And not just that, but you also have to have the determination and the commitment to be true to yourself, to say what's in your heart, and not to be judgmental of self or others. You need to get people with you that you don't think you have to change, that you don't feel critical about, whose peculiarities you can tolerate. It's so much easier when there are no rules that say, "We all meet for dinner at six," and "You cook this week, I cook next week."

Jean Tait: It is essential that women who come together to form community must have worked on all their personal problems and addictions. We must all be as emotionally healthy as we can be, which means we've dealt with our incest memories and cleared them out, we are free of our addictions to alcohol, drugs, caffeine, tobacco, relationships. In other words, we are simply and completely loving ourselves, loving our bodies—and not simply in words, or in our heads, but by showing our bodies, every single day, how much we love them and that we would never abuse them. It is essential that all of us be fully responsible for ourselves, that we assume full responsibility and don't depend or rely on anyone else for our needs.

"Some communities don't work because of hierarchy. Hierarchy destroys things. It just does, it's always going to."

HF: *A lot of intentional communities these days are having problems. From your experience, what do you think prevents communities from working well?*

Jean Tait: Many women who desire community do so because of a need to be taken care of, to have needs met outside of themselves. This, of course, is disastrous, because it sets up a victim/rescuer mode which will destroy a community in short order. *Any* woman who feels she is owed anything, from anyone else, is in trouble, and will create a great deal of disharmony in the community. But when we are in good emotional health, we will be able to allow each and every one of us to be exactly who she is, because, of course, none of us would ever do anything that is intentionally harmful to any other woman.

Sonia Johnson: Some communities don't work because of hierarchy. Hierarchy destroys things. It just does, it's always going to. And yet when you start to say, well then, we can't have any rules, because you can't have any rules without hierarchy, then they start saying oh, but you have to have rules. Anarchy means that you don't have any rules. For me, that is the definition of anarchy: self-government, where there's abundance, and everybody just gives, and makes, and remakes. You do what you want to do all the time, and in doing so, there are goods and services created, and everybody gives and takes. And nobody keeps track; nobody has to be in charge of anything or anybody but themselves.

HF: *At Wildfire, how does it work, everybody doing what they want to do?*

Jean Tait: Well, for example, I love to cook. Cooking for me is a creative outlet. When I felt I *had* to do it, in certain relationships, I started to hate it. Now that I don't have to do it, I'm enjoying it again. So I like to cook, and I like to make things for the women I love. But the nice thing here is that I'm doing it because *I* want to do it. I know that when the food is ready I might ring that bell and nobody'll show up, and that's just fine, because I did it for me. I didn't do it because I wanted praise, or I wanted to be loved more, or respected more, or because I was expected to, or because I was on the schedule. I just did it because I wanted to. And so, whether anybody showed up or not was not even relevant.

Sonia Johnson: It may be that we at Wildfire will be the only ones that'll ever want to do it without rules, but I doubt it. Because I think that women are essentially anarchic, and the time will come when that's clear.

HF: *What about your connection with the Earth, with the place where you live?*

Jean Tait: That's very strong. For example, we are almost totally off the electricity grid; we're solarized, we're just waiting for these new batteries to come into use so we can have those. We've got a windmill that we want to incorporate. Recycling, not taking from the land. You know, I feel she's been taken from so much, that I'm in the place of wanting just to give as much as I can, not to uproot; I don't want to invade that land any more; I really want to change her as little as possible. I don't even want to do a garden in the old way of plowing up the ground. Somehow I don't feel that's what it's about. What I want to do, for now, because there isn't much there, is to just throw seeds out, and let them take where they want to, and then, after they've taken, to leave enough things on the plants so that they fall and go into the ground and then more seeds come up and birds move them around.... That to me is what it's about.

Sonia and I were in California just a few weeks ago, and we were stuck in a traffic jam, and I saw these fields of something, and I said to her, "What *is* that?", and she said, "Rows." And I said, "What?" She said, "Those are rows," and I said, "Of what?" and she said, "It doesn't matter, they're just rows."

Sonia Johnson: I said, "They started out being some plant originally, but now they're just rows. Because," I said, "no plant ever grew naturally in a row, so it is not itself. Whatever it once was, it isn't that any more, it's just rows."

Other women at Wildfire planted our garden, and I said to Jean, "I haven't even been down to the garden, I don't even want to see those rows," and she said, "You know, I've been feeling that way too." It came to both of us at the same time, that we didn't want to do that any more. And then she talked to one of the women who planted the garden, kind of feeling her out about this, saying to her, "Well, I think next year I'll just start a little thing somewhere that's different," and Kathleen said, "I have some thinking about that, too. I don't want to do this." Isn't that interesting? We came to that without talking it over; we each did it on our own.

So next year we will have a free garden. And I think that there will be an abundance. It may take a while for the Earth to really believe us. But I think that when you let her be free, she will just give you back bountifully.

Jean Tait: And I also saw it done; I saw it happen. With my Hopi friend, Chini. In her pueblo, they had a huge communal garden space; somebody came in and roto-tilled it, and plowed and fertilized. Chini refused to have anything to do with it. But she had a space behind her house that was about the size of this room, and it was an incredible little paradise of everything imaginable. She had corn—two kinds of corn, white corn and blue corn— she had beans, she had squashes, she had pumpkins, all growing wildly. Watermelons, unbelieveable watermelons. And lots of weeds and herbs and flowers that were growing in there, in among everybody else.

The year that I was spending so much time with her, there was a major drought. I had to drive by the communal garden every single time I went down there, and it was in bad shape, because the river was so low they couldn't take water from it, so things weren't doing well. A few plants were making it, but overall the garden was dead. And then I'd go to her place and she had *abundance*! She didn't plant anything; she never watered, ever. Never watered, never fed it …. She just loved it, and enjoyed it, and let it do what it wanted to do.

Sonia Johnson: Things that needed more water found the low places where there was more water, and they also invited their companion weeds to come with them, because there are certain weeds that grow with certain other plants, and they shelter them and they shade them, and they mulch them, and they help them hold their water in …. They know how to *do* this.

Jean Tait: That's right, they do it beautifully! I remember that year of drought, one day I got there, and she said, "I need help." She wanted to bring a watermelon in. And she was strong; it was massive—this watermelon, that was growing up the corn! I was very impressed. And her thing was *always*, "If you want to know how to do something, look outside. And not at the 'civilized' world. Take a walk in the mountains." She was right.

HF: *Your friend Chini was from a communal society, the traditional Hopi. Can you say a little more about her?*

Jean Tait: Well, she was a woman who lived just before the Hopi were moved onto the reservation, so she remembered what it was like. The women lived together, with the children; the men were on the periphery. She did not know who her biological mother was. No one did, because the children were all cared for by everyone in the community. She would rarely sleep in the same place two nights in a row, because it was just wherever she was when it was time to go to bed; you just lay down right there with whoever was there. And so she never had that sense of ownership. I remember that for a long time it was confusing to me because she would refer to some woman there as her sister, and I'm thinking, biological sister. In one case she said, "my sister," and it was a woman in her twenties. Now, Chini was over a hundred, and I thought, "This is not possible!" And then I realized that they were all, all of them sisters.

The Hopi were matriarchal, and their way of dealing with—she didn't even talk about conflict—but dealing with things that came up in the community that needed to be discussed, was through non-verbal means. They didn't believe in words, in "processing." They didn't do majority rule, they didn't do compromise. They had no idea what that was about. No such thing. Everything happened as every woman wanted it to be. And my sense about these women was that they were in the same place, able to do that, because they were all in their power, for the most part.

"Hey, community doesn't have to be on the land! You can do it right in the city."

HF: *In the modern world, though, most women are simply not going to be able or willing right now to pick up and leave their present lives to join or form an intentional community. So, what application do these concepts have for the majority of ordinary women, whether lesbian or heterosexual, women of colour or white, urban or rural, privileged or working class, wherever we may live?*

Sonia Johnson: I think that some women in other countries know it already better than we do—the women in Central America, in South America, have done, are doing things like this as you know, at least in their neighborhoods. They're doing communal cooking, communal kitchens, child care—they're beginning to band together *just* to survive. In other words, you're talking about, how can you do this when you have to spend so much time surviving, and I'm saying, Hey, this is survival. This is not a classist, racist thing. The way women can survive best is by doing it together. Whoever we are, wherever we are, women are figuring this out all across the world.

Jean Tait: I was talking with one woman about community and she told me, "You know, I'm not ready for this; I don't know if I'll ever be ready. I really like living in the city." And I said, "Hey, community doesn't have to be on the land! You can do it right in the city." I know women who are in co-op housing, for instance, or they buy a place together, and live together there. I think a lot of us make the connection between community and living on the land, and I don't think that's necessary. There are urban women who want to stay in the city. I know poor women, women who are maybe on public assistance, who have talked about trying to live in close proximity with one another, where they can pool their resources, and, if they have children, help in child care, help relieve each other's burdens in that way too.

HF: *So are you saying, almost no matter what our present circumstances may be, women* can *make the decision to be in community?*

Sonia Johnson: Well, if you've got eight women, and they're each paying rent on something, I mean, if they pooled it, *really* pooled it, that's a land payment! Or a payment on an apartment building in the city! Everybody says, "I don't have enough money," but they're paying a lot already.

Jean Tait: Of course, then they're dealing with the fear that if they do that and it doesn't work out, they're not wanted, then where are they going to go?

Sonia Johnson: They can go right back to where they were, or some other place. I mean, that is always available, it'll be there for a long time. So it just gets down to the point of believing that every one of us is personally responsible to change this world. This is about taking risks out of love for yourself. Because we know full well what our lives are going to be in patriarchy, we know it. There are no surprises there. It's going to be worse and worse for women; there's less and less money—more and more work to get less and less money. That's what we're faced with. All right, if you don't want that—if you love yourself enough, then see if you can do something else. And if you can't, you can always come back and work more and more for less and less.

"If you've got eight women, and they're each paying rent ... if they pooled it, *really* pooled it, that's a land payment! Or a payment on an apartment building in the city!"

HF: *Can you name one key ingredient for building community, building a new world?*

Sonia Johnson: Passion, for ourselves and for each other. And passion about this planet. To be one with it. I want to be in some kind of connection with this planet in a deep way. I want real *intimacy* with her, and I'm passionate about that. I think that will help restore me *and* help restore her, but I'm not *doing* it to restore her. I'm doing it because I love her. The passionate longing for what we're capable of—that's what will move women forward.

Eagle's Nest: A Native Community's Response to Violence

Maureen Miller

Eagle's Nest Stoney Family Shelter in Morley, Alberta, is the first such shelter in the province to be built on an Indian reserve. The fact that it was even built is a major accomplishment. The hope is that the shelter, and the work that goes on inside, will help rid the community of family violence.

Terry Fox is the coordinator of Eagle's Nest. Like most of the women in her community, she's been the victim of abuse, and she knows the extent of the problem. Even so, she's been surprised by the response. There were clients the very day the bunkbeds arrived. And most of the townspeople knew exactly what day that was; the shelter is in the center of town, right beside the tribal police chief's office. Terry Fox says the decision to put the shelter in the center of town was deliberate.

"It was people from outside of the Reserve that were worried that it was in the center," she says. "But we were never worried about it. This symbolizes a healing unit, and when people see the shelter they know that the community is no longer going to tolerate family violence and that we're going to put a stop to it. So it's a good thing that it is where it is, so everybody can see it and know what it means."

The shelter staff believe native ways are what is needed to help the women heal themselves. Jackie, one of the first women at Eagle's Nest, has been through several shelters, but they were always miles away from her home, always run by people from a different culture, speaking a different language. She says in those places she could heal her body, but not her soul. "The white counsellors, they would never be able to help me out. There's such a culture difference in our backgrounds. Native people are brought up in a certain way, and they need to be with their own people. They understand what you're going through, and how you were brought up and how it can help you."

John Snow, Chief of the Stoney for well over twenty-five years, agrees. He says there is a lot of healing that needs to be done. "I think a lot of that healing has to come from a native point of view, native way. The aboriginal thinking is quite different. We have the mountain hot springs that we go to for healing. Where are they today? They're tourist resorts. We can't even go there. Our sacred areas are taken from us, so we're corralled in a little reservation, and when we have problems, people wonder why."

"Now it's out in the open ... and the community sees that we'll no longer tolerate the violence, as a whole community. I am proud of that ... we have the guts to face it."

Chief Snow points out that native people have been robbed of their way of life. Unemployment on the reserve is at a whopping eighty per cent. Alcohol and drug abuse is rampant. Family violence is one of the results.

The community has a two-pronged strategy to deal with this: the shelter for the women, education for the men. Terry Fox says, "I think that the men aren't feeling as threatened any more, because we're not out to get the men. We want to help all—we want to take a wholistic approach. And you can't just fix one side of the problem and leave the other, so we've hired an outreach worker to work with the men."

The outreach worker, Bruce Dixon, counsels the partners of the women who show up at the shelter. He says some of the men don't even know that when a man hits a woman, it's wrong. "They ask me, what is family violence? They don't really know. It's just that they might have done it before, and it's OK for them because nothing's been done about it. So we're doing community workshops about family violence. Now that the shelter's here, and the women know that something can be done about it, they're starting to think more about what abuse really means."

"Now it's out in the open," says Terry Fox, "and the community sees that we'll no longer tolerate the violence, as a whole community. I am proud of that. We have a problem, we have the guts to face it, and we're dealing with it. I think it might take a few years; you can't expect everybody to change instantly. It's going to be slow, and we're going to have to take it step by step. But it's going to come."

13

Krutsio:
A Desert Metamorphosis

Adrian Aguirre

Krutsio is a small intentional community in the desert wilderness on the Pacific Coast of Baja California in Mexico. The human population of Krutsio shares its "ejido"—its common land—with the surrounding marine and desert ecosystems—the unique cacti and other vegetation of the Baja Peninsula, and local wildlife, including deer, coyotes, seals and migrating grey whales.

The community's core group is a family of four; Adrian Aguirre and Gabriela Lugo moved from Mexico City in 1976, and other members have come and gone at various stages during its development. Krutsio describes itself as the nucleus of "a cellular community—that is, a social cell of the future planetary organism which incorporates the best of rural and urban traditions. The cellular community is a new social unit based on psychological, economic and ecological guidelines." Krutsio sees a need for emerging cellular communities to interconnect, and it is part of the network of the Federation of Egalitarian Communities.

All the buildings and facilities have been built and are maintained by Krutsians using mainly local materials; the same is true of the eleven and a half kilometres of rocky desert track leading to the nearest road—itself little more than a bumpy trail of dust through the arid mountains. To visit Krutsio is to arrive in a new world, a world where concepts of natural beauty, of human ingenuity, and of possibility itself are transformed.

The rugged beauty and extreme isolation at Krutsio both inspire and demand self-reliance and creativity. The following article is adapted from Krutsio's publication, "The Principles of Cellularism/Los Principios del Celularismo."

We see our community as part of a progression in the role of humans on the planet. Our distant ancestors lived in natural communities, as part of their ecosystems, in harmony with plants and animals in a defined environment. Humanity was just emerging—few, dispersed, close to the Earth and struggling for survival. Present-day industrial society has vandalized community, with ecosystems under intense attack by adolescent, semi-conscious humans. Competition and exploitation prevail, bolstered by arrogance posing as knowledge. There is imbalance and fragmentation, big cities, big wars, consumerism, pollution, language imperialism. Humanity plagues the Earth.

Our vision of tomorrow sees natural community healed and refined by means of the harmonious influence of mature human consciousness. In this new cellular society, made up of interconnected cellular communities, cooperation prevails; wisdom and love counsel deliberate frugality, human unity and peace, vitalization and healing of the Earth.

The realization of this vision can come about through a process of global metamorphosis: the transformation of a system from one stable form to a qualitatively different form which incorporates its own parts, like a caterpillar becoming a butterfly. The initial stage—an exhausted, decaying, futureless system—nevertheless contains within itself the seed and the ingredients for the stage that eventually emerges—an alternative system which grows in as the initial system fades out.

As a strategy for social change, metamorphosis can be profound, efficient and rapid without being violent. The most powerful force for social change is that of example. Joining with other like-minded people in interconnecting communities enables everyone to support each other in creating real social change, which flows from the bottom up, induced by individual change. Such changes culminate in the transformation of societal organization and structure. Cellular communities can be the seeds of sustainable alternatives, in a process of metamorphosis on a global scale.

At Krutsio we try to practise many interrelated principles that we see as necessary for this process: pacifism and non-violence; equality; diversity and balance; organization; egalitarian interconnection and exchange; integration of theory and practice; use of Esperanto as a global language; experimentation; persistence; cooperation and sharing; healthy living. In the context of bioregional community, a number of our principles can be highlighted: living with nature; frugality; self-sufficiency; multifunctionality and overlapping; respect for life; optimal utilization of local resources; revitalization; use of renewable cyclo-energies; appropriate, non-polluting practices and technologies; recycling; and the production of quality goods.

Living with nature, rather than against her, means basing human actions on natural processes. It requires knowing nature and how our actions affect her, and respecting her inherent wisdom. To begin with, it is most sensible to try to affect as little as possible. When we walk to the beach or up the mountain, we follow paths so as to leave undisturbed as much of the rocky desert ground as possible, allowing its sparse and delicate vegetation to help protect it from erosion. Through knowing and respecting nature, we can grow with her rather than at her expense.

"Frugality is not poverty; it is a mid-point between scarcity and opulence."

Among other things, this implies *frugality*. Frugality means consuming the minimum—only what is necessary, and utilizing to the maximum—taking full advantage of what we do use. For example, in the desert, water is precious; we use sea water for bathing, laundry and dishes, and re-use it as appropriate, reserving our solar-distilled water for drinking, cooking, and watering our plants. We don't consume much at Krutsio; instead, we "chew and digest" things well, and we generate a minimum amount of garbage. Without a heavy load of possessions to acquire and protect, we can use much of our own energy for growing and living. Frugality is not poverty; it is a mid-point between scarcity and opulence.

The community collectively provides the basic goods and services it needs to survive: water, food, energy, shelter, basic education, health care and maintenance. This *self-sufficiency* saves energy and money, enables us to go on living if we ever become temporarily isolated from the rest of society, and ensures our dignity and independence. Self-sufficient communities are not easily subjugated in return for food! Since more is required for plentiful living than just meeting our basic survival needs, we also produce exchangeable goods and services—for example, *nori*, which we harvest from the sea, seashell jewellery and artwork, writing and organizational skills. These exports permit us to import complementary goods and services from outside the community. But the ideal economic exchange has more of a social than a profit motive. Our idea is not to sell a lot in order to buy a lot, but to channel our abundance to cover our scarcities.

Another recognized ecological principle is the complementary dual concept of *multifunctionality and overlapping*, that is, trying to take advantage of all possible functions for each thing, and at the same time, trying to have each necessary function covered by more than one person or object. Our bodies give us examples of this ingenuity in the design of organisms: a mouth is good for eating, speaking, singing, whistling, laughing, kissing, biting, holding, etc. If we go blind in one eye, we can still see with the other; if we hurt our hand, we can use the other one. In our community, each person does several kinds of jobs, while each job can be done by several people; we all have a back-up in each function. All our roofs collect what little rainwater may come, but we also produce our regular supply of drinking water by solar distillation of water from the sea.

"In our community, each person does several kinds of jobs, while each job can be done by several people; we all have a back-up in each function."

Respect for life means recognizing that all living creatures are connected, and treating them as our sisters and brothers. For us, it entails allowing other life forms to live, giving them the benefit of the doubt,

---

The Michigan Womyn's Worker Village

We Want The Music Company

The Michigan Womyn's Music Festival is created each year by a group of womyn working together. We are a gathering of womyn of many diverse cultures and experiences who share a common bond—our desire to live a week of womyn-centered life. The concept and structure of the Festival is built on the premise that we all provide the necessary village services for each other.

Through the fall, winter and early spring, four womyn work full-time planning and organizing hundreds of pieces of the foundation for another year's homecoming. But the magic begins in June when we first step back on to the land and mark the beginning of this year's Worker Village.

First there are two. They drive through the Front Gate as they have so many times before, moving slowly along Lois Lane, nodding in silence at the jade-hued return of the ferns .... Over to the wheelchair area to measure off the path for this year's wheelway addition .... Stop on the way to Acoustic Stage to allow a porcupine her leisurely way across the road. And so it begins.

not hurting or killing them unnecessarily. It means taking our vital energy as directly from the sun as possible. Plankton and seaweed "eat" sunlight; some fish eat plankton, other fish eat those fish, we humans can eat all sorts of things. But since to make a pound of biomass at each level of the food chain requires about ten pounds from the previous level, the closer to the sun we eat, the less we have to kill.

Respect for life also means killing with love whenever killing is necessary. That is, other things being equal, we should sacrifice less complex organisms; it is better to kill soybean plants for protein than to kill cows. We should cause the least possible suffering in the killing, sacrifice only organisms that have already reproduced themselves, and avoid endangering any species. Finally, respect involves positive action as well, treating others (including other species) as we would like to be treated.

In mid-July, a half dozen womyn set up a makeshift work centre with water jugs and tool boxes. They walk through the forest with no hint of the activity to come. One team will sight off a familiar cherry tree and large maple, and knowingly dig down into the earth until they carefully reach in and pull up electric cable buried away last fall.

Later that week, the first crew, made up of a few cooks, carpenters, plumbers and tent raisers roll past the Front Gate and set up the simple camp that makes the center of the Worker Village. We sit comfortably around a small firepit where oatmeal bubbles early in the morning and a womon flips pancakes on a large campfire skillet. We have the quiet of our own company which we treasure for these few days, and the happy anticipation of what is about to bloom again.

"The gift has been living together in these peaceful Michigan woodlands as we find our harmony with Mother Nature."

By Sunday when the first 120 womyn of the Long Crews arrive to work on the different set-up crews—Lace Hardware, Land, Plumbing, Carpentry, Mechanics, Transportation, Signs, Communications, Worker Kitchen, First Aid, Inventory, Massage, Child-care, Electrics, Worker Support and Office— we have the makings of our Village which will be home for the month.

We humans are responsible for the place we live in. At Krutsio we try to optimize our use of all the resources from our home place, both for self-sufficiency and for exchange. For example, we build with the stone of the desert that surrounds us; create and decorate with shells; bathe with sea water; eat seaweed, fish, shellfish and the fruit of cacti; convert the wind into electricity; slide and play in the sand of the beach; orient our outhouse to the magnificent view of the sea. Taking advantage and *making full use of local resources* is very different from exploiting or destroying; it helps to increase the quantity and quality of life on our planet.

Another aspect of this responsibility for our home place is to promote the development of life according to the potential of each ecosystem. The outstanding criteria for this *vitalization* include the naturalness, diversity, complementarity, stability, efficiency and quantity of life in

Each morning the breakfast crew from Gal's Diner calls the first meal. Womyn wander out of tent homes tucked into the aspen groves that make up worker camping. Within a few days, the towel racks appear at the showers across from the Witches Clearing. The Belly Bowl comes together where we eat our meals, have dinner meetings to share tales of the day's work, and meet for games and talent shows or dancing later in the evening. Late at night you might see a small group of womyn walking up Easy Street, listening for owls, watching the skyful of constellations or thinking of the laughter which will ring through the campgrounds in a few weeks.

In these easy, relaxed days, womyn spread out over the land in small crews, wood-chipping thousands of feet of paths, fitting pipe and digging trenches for runs of water to the kitchen, the showers, the bubbler fountains that will offer a cool drink on a hot day mid-Festival. A womon stands at the foot of a large oak tree and calls up directions to a partner hanging in a tree sling, pruning deadwood over campgrounds.

Ten days before the Festival, the Short Crews arrive, rounding out the crews of the areas which provide support services to all the womyn on staff. Dinner meetings need to be translated in American Sign Language, Spanish, French, German, Norwegian, and Russian. Tent Day arrives and the Lace Crew leads a hundred womyn in raising seventy-five tents. Womyn who never

each place. In general, the more of all these qualities, the better. If one's home place is a natural fertile ecosystem, we must respect and support that in every way we know. A natural desert ecosystem, like that surrounding Krutsio, presents a challenge of vitalization: with constructive human ingenuity there could be more life here. In the case of ecosystems which have been or are being devastated by human action, our obligation is to restore life. This vitalization is our way to repay the planet.

The development of industrial society has been based on the use of nonrenewable, dangerous and polluting energies.The use of these external energies amplifies our capabilities, but giving more energy to fools amplifies madness. Frugal societies don't require enormous amounts of energy in any case. Using *cyclo-energies*—sources of energy

---

thought they would hold a sledge hammer are swinging them with confidence and methodical team work.

International Rug Day follows as an all-camp event. Tugging and stretching carpets into paths from centre to centre, we lay the web of the bigger village which is about to come to life around us.

Just before the last weekend, the final hundred and fifty womyn arrive for the During Fest Crews to set up and staff all the areas in Festieland: Box Office, Parking, Shuttle, Traffic, Orientation, Oasis, Sober Support, Community Center, Over-40s, Womyn of Colors, One World, the Womb, the Stages, Child-care Camps, Festiewear, the Store and the Saints.

Signs come out of the Signz Studio and punctuate everything. Tables and chairs move into tents, colorful lights get strung through trees, pounds of poster board meet colored marking pens, scaffolding sections get swung into the sky. The womyn who have travelled from all over the world to build a festival together, realize that they have built a family of workers who have laughed, cried, processed, joked, sung, taught and learned with each other. The goal has always been preparing the place for the Festival to happen when the thousands more womyn come in August. The gift has been living together in these peaceful Michigan woodlands as we find our harmony with Mother Nature.

that are renewable and non-polluting—enables us to live in harmony with nature and with a peaceful conscience.

At Krutsio, we use a solar dryer to preserve food, solar water heaters for washing and bathing, solar distillation to produce potable water from sea water, and a wind generator supplemented by photovoltaic cells as sources for the small amounts of electricity we need. We also use muscular and mechanical energy a lot, with hand tools for building, repairs and maintenance, a pedal machine for grinding, and bicycles for some of our transportation.

The natural communities which existed originally did not know pollution. Everything was recycled in a natural way. Now pollution is everywhere, interfering with the planet's life processes, and by producing or using polluting products, we become accomplices in its destructiveness. The solution is not to go backwards, but to make sure we consume only what is truly necessary, produced by means of *appropriate technologies* which are renewable and minimally polluting, recycling what we use.

Natural processes tend to form cycles, which would repeat over and over, practically without end, if it were not for humans. We humans have become the most prominent obstacles in natural cycles; we are experts in making non-recyclable what was once recyclable! To survive, we have to reintegrate ourselves into the natural cycles of which we ourselves are a part. Instead of interfering with them, we can assist them by means of *recycling*.

"In the case of ecosystems which have been or are being devastated by human action, our obligation is to restore life. This vitalization is our way to repay the planet."

Recycling has a number of different aspects. At Krutsio, when we categorize our trash resources, we separate organic wastes, paper, bottles, cans, etc., and keep them to be used later in different ways. We participate in the natural cycle of nutrients by converting organic wastes and excrement into compost for the use of plants, which eventually provide food. Staging of resource use enables one resource to be used several times; for example, we save and reuse water by rinsing with it first, then washing semi-dirty things, and lastly using the dirtied water for the dirtiest things. And we maintain and repair items to prolong their useful life, rather than replacing them as soon as they show signs of wear.

In industrial society, things tend to be made hastily, to be consumed in great quantity, and for the sake of profit. In cellular communities, *quality products* are made with pleasure to satisfy real needs. We try to make our products simple, effective, inexpensive, efficient, beautiful, durable, reuseable, easily maintained, and with recyclable component parts.

"Using *cyclo-energies*—sources of energy that are renewable and non-polluting—enables us to live in harmony with nature and with a peaceful conscience."

Krutsio's attempt to change the world has so far been tiny in quantitative terms, but it is nonetheless meaningful in terms of metamorphosis. Rather than be part of the problem, we choose to to be a small part of the solution.

14

A People of Place

Van Andruss and Eleanor Wright

Eleanor Wright and Van Andruss live among friends in the interior mountains of British Columbia. They are active in forest defense, grassroots democracy and regional organizing. They are two of the coeditors of Home! A Bioregional Reader, *and helped organize the third North American Bioregional Congress, held in British Columbia in 1988. In this article, they describe seasonal and daily life in their community, a valley reinhabited by people with a bioregional vision.*

Tomorrow night is full moon and Winter Solstice both. The old year is ending and the new year just beginning. Yes, there will be celebrations. The people of this valley will get together; there will be music, dancing, feasting—and beautiful desserts!

At some point in the evening, we will form a circle and speak to each other, all of us together. We'll acknowledge the presence of elders and special guests. We'll remember friends who could not be present; we'll honor the household hosting the occasion. We'll mention the value of the food and the preparers of the food, and we'll thank the Earth that produced it.

Gifts will be exchanged. These are not Christmas presents, they are Solstice presents, intended to celebrate the rhythms of our fruitful planet and our good friendships with each other.

Ours is a community of place. It is composed not only of human partners, but of ponderosas and firs, bunchgrasses, birds and cold-running creeks. Within this web of beings we are attempting to make ourselves a home. We are being shaped in our character, diet, occupations and physical person by these crazy slopes and the weather

105

and winds that blow overhead on their journey to the Interior. Every day we are being taught the conditions to be met.

For thousands of years before the arrival of Europeans, native peoples lived in this region. They returned seasonally to this valley for its excellent hunting, for furs and berries. Some of the grandchildren of these ancestors have befriended us, and what remains of their ancient culture continues to inspire.

"Ours is a community of place. …We are being shaped in our character, diet, occupations and physical person by these crazy slopes and the weather and winds that blow overhead on their journey to the Interior."

It's fair to say that, in a sense, we want to become native too; that is definitely the direction of our hundred-year plan. We mean to stick together, stay here, and in the manner of community close the gap between ourselves and the land.

The fashion for civilized North Americans is to be forever on the move. No doubt in the past there was good reason to pull up stakes and get away from narrow-minded places of origin. Now, however, with the health of the planet rapidly declining, it makes sense to settle down and be peaceful somewhere, to cultivate, restore and protect some actual patch of earth.

We reside here on the edge of the empire, on the periphery of the commercial grid. Besides the narrow strip of human habitation, there is no sign of civilization. Summers, we pack into the bush exploring our watershed, camping beside lakes or in the open, rolling, high meadows. How vast and beautiful it all is, containing every sort of wisdom if only we can learn to receive it. Our familiarity with the rocks, the animals, the plants is deepening. Our children can recite the names of the wildflowers and the uses of some of the medicinal herbs. Little by little we become indigenous. Certainly it must take generations to ripen as a culture and take root in a new world.

*

Picking knapweed in July. Hot sun. Fifteen or twenty adults, kids too. We're pulling weed near the dam where the ground has been scarified by heavy construction. Altogether we are responsible for over fifteen miles of roadside, fifty feet on either side. Only a community of workers could handle such an area. As it is, we spend about ten days per season at the job. We have nothing against knapweed exactly; we're pulling it because if we don't, the local forestry office threatens to spray with herbicide, and we don't want poisons leaching into the river. Wherever possible we line up side by side and clank away with our shovels, gossiping, joking, or talking philosophy as we move along. Without that cool breeze sweeping through, we'd be miserable.

"One reason for living in place is to defend an area from exploitation by The Machine. Where people are not, the field is clear for commercial interests."

At lunch we take time to sit under the trees. The kids come running back from the wading pond at the foot of the dam. Out come the pickles, bread and cheese. After a while, since we're all together, we take up a little business, talking about some of the public issues that concern us.

A helicopter flies overhead. Counting trees, most likely. Hovering, taking an inventory of remaining resources. Such attitudes seem so alien to our hopes. Already our valley is a remnant of its former glory. One reason for living in place is to defend an area from exploitation by The Machine. Where people are not, the field is clear for commercial interests.

Forestry is a main issue with us during this period. We are involved in a Land Resource Use Plan, struggling to get a long-term plan for our whole watershed. We are labouring to educate our district forestry experts to the notion of ecological sustainablility and the requirements of biodiversity. We demand the kind of management that does not destroy the forest with all its inhabitants.

So, harboring in the shade of the trees, we catch up on recent developments relating to the protection of our home place. Some lie back and rest for a spell. In the near distance, unbelievable cliffs, sheer walls of gray rock greet the eye. Leaning fir trees perched on ledges smile down on us, and from one crevice high up, a thin waterfall drifts and curls in the afternoon breeze.

*

The people of this community began drifting into the valley over fifteen years ago. We came from all over the continent, from different homes, neighborhoods and institutions. All of us are self-reliant characters; almost all come from backgrounds of rebellion or dissatisfaction with the system. How such a mix of oddballs should have congregated in one narrow valley makes a story in itself. How we could have thought out and acted upon extensive agreements, as we have done, must be regarded as a marvel of communication. Yet something clicked among us and we saw the benefit of working together towards common goals.

When we look around the circle tomorrow night, we'll see a gathering of well-fed, well-knit pioneers who are our great friends, but who were not born creators of alternative culture. As ordinary North Americans, we are in no way especially equipped to carry out utopian visions. All of us are experiencing the growing pains of a transition, and not one of us is perfectly wise or wholly correct in our behaviours. Nevertheless, we are beautiful to behold. Great talents exist among us. We're capable of darn near anything. We are of that global tribe called "the people," and the people have always built, dismantled and rebuilt worlds.

"The community as a whole is our principal thinking group. There is Council, our central organizing body, in which we get together once a month, form our circle and discuss community concerns."

Most of our common life is founded on trust, goodwill, generosity and patience. The love underneath is what has held our little world together, and still does. For the most part, whatever methods we have used to become united have been informal. The ways of Mother Nature are not formal, and neither are the domestic affairs of barnyard and potato patch. Imagination tends to find its way around formal or bureaucratic obstacles to action, thriving in a liberal atmosphere.

This doesn't mean, however, that we lack methods of ordering our collective activity. Where we can, we proceed by collective intelligence, and the community as a whole is our principal thinking group. There is Council, our central organizing body, in which we get together once a month, form our circle and discuss community concerns. To cover all our doings and all important personal issues would be impossible; internal affairs are complicated and have public repercussions. We handle what is uppermost. Many of our topics are business-like. We schedule events—the women's circle, the men's circle, the meeting of the ecological society, the food co-op. Strategies are devised and things are planned in some detail, with actions carried out on a voluntary basis. Without Council, it's hard to envision how our association could move forward.

Of course, the way to tribal unity is hard, and difficulties persistently arise. We are in a period when North American consumer society seems to be reaching its highest peak. Many people have been hurt by the system; they feel bruised all over, and trust is not easy to come by. The acquisition of private property accentuates tendencies towards individualism. Titles of land ownership isolate us. Money, sex and male dominance are other possible stumbling blocks to genuine community. There is not one man or woman in our circle who has not been shaken to consciousness of sexist attitudes and behaviors.

These and other problems flare up in conflict, and when conflict arises, people lose their sense of balance. Communities are no exception to the rule. Conflict will emerge and it becomes a matter of how people deal with it. Without a means of conflict resolution, no community can hold out for long. Our response is to be developing the process of consensus as fast as we can. Members of the community have taken courses in non-violence, facilitation, mediation and co-counselling. Despite recurrent breakdowns in relations, most of us have managed to stay put, and we continue to extend ourselves to reach sound agreements and settle differences that become hot.

Perhaps the consensus process within the full Council is a way to begin, for the people assembled is the only body approaching wholeness, standing for the best interests of all parties, with that degree of detachment capable of settling disputes, and indifferent to no one's pain. Meanwhile, we value compassion, flexibility, and a sense of humor.

*

At one time, not so long ago, our dream of an ideal alternative kept us up all night talking. Now we are actualizing our dreams. We think about land trusts, about better organizing our informal economy, about the restoration work that will bring plant and animal life back to the eroded hillsides.

"Building a new world is a grand-scale idea, but the actual work is humble, attentive to detail, and carried on at the scale of the familiar."

The turning of the seasons gives us our basic rhythm. Spring calls us to the gardens; in the fall we harvest our crops, preserve and pack them away in the root cellars, eating our way through them during the winter months. The chores give us a set of steady habits, and normal life proceeds around the simple tasks involved in taking care of things. We support the chickens who in turn support us; we raise hay for the goats who feed us. We produce our own food, educate the children, make our own entertainment, and generate our electricity from the mountain streams, creating an alternative to the dependencies of consumer society. But it all takes doing, and a person is kept awfully busy. Building a new world is a grand-scale idea, but the actual work is humble, attentive to detail, and carried on at the scale of the familiar.

Like bioregional people everywhere, we aspire to membership in the web of ecosystems converging in our local place. We expect to fit in with the species, the water sources, the soil types surrounding us. In community we see our best hope. The promise, already partially realized, is that in this way we will find wholeness and happiness.

Tomorrow night, then, we will celebrate our place and our people. Under a full moon, we will mark the arrival of the Winter Solstice, honor our relations, and beat the planetary drums!

15

Daughters of Growing Things

A conversation between
Rachel L. Bagby and Rachel E. Bagby

This dialogue tells of an ongoing effort to maintain mutually nurturing relationships with nature, human and elemental, in the midst of a low- and no-income urban village community of about 5000 people. Located within the city of Philadelphia, this urban village functions as a self-governing political unit, and has several half-acre plots that are worked by the community.

Rachel L. Bagby owes her life to the stories of the women in her family, and is dedicated to preserving them. A graduate of Stanford Law School, she is a writer, composer, and advocate for environmental justice. Her life work is to co-create a sustainable, land-based multi-cultural community. Rachel Edna Bagby, her mother, is an elder who nurtures life on Earth. She founded and directs the Philadelphia Community Rehabilitation Corporation (PCRC), which operates housing, employment and literacy programs as well as the gardens described in the conversations from which the following excerpts are taken.

Rachel L. Bagby says, "It is essential to have Momma tell her stories in her own, inimitable voice. Much of her power in the community comes from her way with people, and much of that way is communicated in her manner of speaking."

Mother: See, what give me the idea to do this, is I just got sick and tired of walking by weeds. Absolutely a disgrace to me. If weeds can grow in there, something else can grow also. And you have the weeds taller than I am. People be afraid to go by Twenty-First Street. That's where we had to go to the store, and people would snatch pocketbooks and run over you, and you couldn't find them in the weeds. So that's how we got started with that.

Daughter: How did you get people interested? You just went around and talked to people?

Mother: Like door-to-door campaigning; door-to-door education.

Daughter: I'm wondering about how the city got involved.

Mother: We approached the city to help us, because we found out they could help us do a lot. That's how I got in with them. Anything that I think can give us a hand, because we need a lot of help out here. But if you don't ever ask for it, you won't get it.

Daughter: How much land do you have?

Mother: I think it's about five acres, all the different lots we have. They were all empty lots, and we just got them, we asked for them in order to make the place look better than growing a whole lot of weeds. We just grow something that's more useful—food and flowers. Make it beautiful. And the food is outta sight. Rather than to grow weeds. Why sit and grow weeds when you can do something with it? So this is what we did, and it's working, and it's spreading. We have a meeting now every month.

Daughter: How did you prepare the land? And what was the original shape? Wasn't there glass and other debris to clear out?

Mother: We just took hoes and rakes and stuff and raked it. Dug it as deep as the plants will grow, and raked all that stuff and put it out. We dug with something called a grub hoe, and just paid some boys for just going in and digging it up. Tole them, "Just dig it as deep as the food will grow."

Daughter: How deep is that?

Mother: About as deep as my leg. Two or three feet. What we did, we did that and then we asked for top soil and had folks go out in the park and get the horse manure from the park. Woodside Park. The stables—the drippings from the horses. Stable compost, they call it. We go out there and get it and it don't cost anything. Just go out there and haul it. It makes such good dirt. You heap it up, all that stuff. That's how your crop grows.

"What grows in the ground, what grows on top, what good for blood, what good for different things. A lot of adults don't have any idea."

Daughter: You said you paid some boys to do it?

Mother: We had two or three boys and we paid them to dig it up for us. We didn't have a plow. I know how we used to do it in the South, turn it with the turnplow and two horses. But we didn't have the turnplow here, so we just paid the men to dig it up and dig it deep and they had to dig it right. It didn't take them long. Took 'em like two days.

Daughter: Who did the planting?

Mother: Well, I supervised the planting. Most everybody helped.

Daughter: Do you plant from seeds?

Mother: You plant from seeds, some of them were planted from seeds and some of them were plants we bought. The ones that we couldn't get enough plants up from seeds, we bought.

Daughter: And you timed it all based on the moon?

Mother: Yes. I always plant according to the moon. According to the light I know when to plant.

Daughter: How much did it cost you for the seeds, the plants, the hoes, the other equipment, paying the boys? How much do you think all that cost?

Mother: Well, the land was about $1000 for the land. And we put the fence up. I think that wire fence was $1,300—cyclone fence. Then we used the boys two days and I paid them, that was $3 an hour. There was two boys, $3 an hour for sixteen hours. The seeds run you less than a dollar a pack, the plants about $1.50 to $2.00. Say, about $10 worth of plants, say, $10 for the seeds. That's just an estimate, now. We bought about $200 worth of equipment, but we don't buy that every year.

Daughter: Well, you don't buy the land or the fence every year either. It looks like your yearly costs are $20 for the seeds and plants.

Mother: Yes, you can put about $20 or $25 for the year. For the seeds themselves, and the plants. They just use the equipment over and over again.

Daughter: That $25 feeds how many people for how long?

Mother: About twelve households for one season. Vegetables year-round. During the summer we eat a lot out of there, we don't have to can it. I told you, vegetables we don't buy.

Daughter: What happens at your meetings? You said the meetings have been growing.

Mother: We trying to get them to realize how much they save by doing this. And spread it. Because the city has so many vacant lots so they can plant these things. This is what we're trying to get them to do, and show them the value of doing this.

Daughter: Who comes to these meetings?

Mother: Just people that're interested in planting gardens. We had forty-nine last week. Neighborhood people. And now we're letting them see how the food looks canned, and also how it tastes.

Daughter: It sounds like a real educational program. What else are you planning?

Mother: Well, we're planning to do more gardening. Add a little bit more each year. Gardening, shared housing, and regular housing. We're also getting tutoring for literacy, starting to teach some people how to read and get jobs.

Daughter: Do you still have training programs for kids to get employment?

Mother: Yes, we still have that job bank, that's what we call that.

Daughter: How do you think what you do relates to ecology, relates to the Earth? How do you talk about that?

Mother: Well, I talk about it like I always do, 'cause this is where you see the real nature of the universe. The real one, without ... before it's transformed into different things. Because even children don't have the least idea of the food they eat. What grows in the ground, what grows on top, what good for blood, what good for different things. A lot of adults don't have any idea. So that's how I relate it to everyday living.

You get firsthand ... Everybody get a firsthand look at real nature. You can see it come up, you can see it grow and you see how it grows, and see it dies if you don't take care of it.

"You look at the fingernails and know they're too long to do any work. So that's the resistance you get, 'cause we are uneducated to the facts."

Daughter: What kind of resistance have you met?

Mother: People not wantin' to work. They don't want to get their hands dirty. They don't wanna dig down and get the carrots from the ground, they don't want to get the turnips from the ground. That's dirt. When they get it it's in the store and they clean, so to speak. So a lot of them rather go to the store and get it. I say, "How long it's been in that store? You can get it right from here and clean it, put it right in your pot or eat it like it is. Put it in your salad and you get it real, all the vitamins."

So you have resistance, people say, I can't bend down, can't bend over, or my fingernails too long. They don't tell you that, but you look at the fingernails and know they're too long to do any work. So that's the resistance you get, 'cause we are uneducated to the facts. And not just in that, but in a lot of things. We just don't seem to understand.

But I feel as though our children would better understand how to take care of things and would have a better feeling of the things around them. It begins when you're small, really.

Daughter: Do you work with children a lot in the garden?

Mother: I love to, yes. I generally have them in there and showing them the grass from the weeds and from the plants and how it looks and how they grow, too. The grass grows, too. The weeds grow, too. That's part of nature. They say, "What good are they?" "This can be fertilizer for next year." "What!? Weeds!?" "You let them sit there and rot and that replenish the Earth. See, everything has a cycle." See, those the kinda things.

You do that with children, all of them will not end up in jail. Some of 'em come out all right.

"If you can appreciate the Earth, you can appreciate the beauty of yourself. ...And if I learned to take care of that, I'll also take care of myself and help take care of others."

Daughter: Why do you think showing them living things helps them straighten up?

Mother: I think it will help them to appreciate the beauty of the Earth, and of nature. If you can appreciate the Earth, you can appreciate the beauty of yourself. Even if this has beauty, I, too, have beauty. And if I learned to take care of that, I'll also take care of myself and help take care of others. See, taking care of yourself and appreciating yourself is the first step.

Daughter: And how about the old folks who work on the garden?

Mother: I think we had a ninety-year-old man working in the garden, but he not able to come any more. But he worked 'til he was ninety-something years old. We give him a plaque for being the oldest gardener that we had. And he had the prettiest garden we had. He couldn't read, but he'd have you read it to him and he would catch it as you read it and go do just what you say. Like the directions on the paper how you plant? You read it out to him, he won't miss a thing. He go right on and do it.

Daughter: So everybody has a place?

Mother: Right. That's it. That's how it's done, but it takes a lot of time and a lot of ... It takes a lot of time with these people to counsel them. You can't do it in a hurry and you can't do it one time and you can't limit the times that you hafta do it. You have to do it until it gets done. That's all.

Daughter: But you do see some results?

Mother: Well, yes, you see a good bit of results. I saw a good bit of results this summer when we were putting those plants out. They said the plants were not gonna stay. The children themselves didn't destroy any of the plants. They watched out for the plants. And they enjoyed the street. They played ball but none of the ball broke those plants. They watched out for it. Close as it is. They watched out for it and that was marvelous.

"When you have your vision, that's one step; as you go through one, it'll go to the next step. And you follow it, nothing gonna be unturned; everything will work in place."

When you have your vision, that's one step; as you go through one, it'll go to the next step. And you follow it, nothing gonna be unturned; everything will work in place.

16

"Be What You've Come Here For"

Kay Chornook

In September 1989, the Temagami Wilderness Society (TWS) established a blockade of a logging road extension then under construction through the land of the Teme Augama Anishnabai in Northeastern Ontario. The blockade was the culmination of years of frustrating effort by environmentalists to save this magnificent wilderness ecosystem from destruction by logging and mining interests, and to support the Teme Augama Anishnabai in their generations-old struggle to regain their homeland.

Kay Chornook, a landscaper from Charlton, just north of Temagami, has been involved in this struggle for a number of years as a supporter and friend of the native people and as a member of the board of directors of TWS. She has also worked with the Monte Verde Conservation League in Costa Rica. When Kay shakes those trees, she's prepared for the coconuts to fall!

In the following article, Kay describes the community that formed on the shores of Lake Wakimika, as what began as a weekend Camp-In turned into a seven-week province-wide campaign to insist that the government halt the destruction of the Temagami wilderness and finally deal with the issues there in a just and sustainable manner.

"Know your human right ... be what you've come here for."

—Sting.

In the fall of 1989 we knew our human right and took it to its ultimate—non-violent civil disobedience. Hundreds of environmentalists and supporters of aboriginal rights were part of a remote beach camp on Wakimika Lake in the Temagami region, and many of those people were arrested for blockading construction of the Red Squirrel Road extension. The completed road would be an expressway into the heart of n'Daki Menan, the homeland of the Teme Augama Anishnabai, a remaining piece of wilderness in a land violated by those who believe it is their right to dispose of it recklessly.

In the months of planning for the action, I don't think that any of us imagined what would happen in those beautiful northern woods: a community formed that was centered among the tents and around the campfire, but extended to the communications centre 25 miles away near the highway, to the surrounding northern towns, to the offices of Northwatch in North Bay and TWS in Toronto, and throughout the network of environmentalists in Ontario.

As I spent Saturday, September 16, 1989, ferrying people by motorboat in groups of two or three up Diamond Lake to the last portage into Wakimika, I had no way of knowing what was gelling at the beachsite we had adopted for the weekend "camp-in." When we finally arrived in the dark with the last group, the flickering light of the campfires revealed a crowd of more than two hundred, the result of our steady day-long ferry system as well as of the constant arrival of seaplanes and canoes.

On awakening Sunday morning, the long beach was decorated with dozens of tents that looked like colorful mushrooms that had popped up overnight. We spent the day in a large circular meeting on the beach, with instruction in civil disobedience, and discussion of our action plans for the following day. Facilitating that meeting was a challenge. The group included northern community members, southern environmentalists, grandmothers, Earth Firsters, mainstream activists, anarchists, international participants, children and media people. Few of us had any experience of this kind of action, and we all envisioned it in different ways; it scared many, fired up most, and evoked powerful emotions. Add to this the justified paranoia about "plants"—agitators, informers—and concern about media access to the discussions, and the meeting had every reason to dissolve into confusion and confrontation. But somehow we managed not only to get through the agenda about the next day's action, but also to inspire a large number of people to forsake their responsibilities back home to stay on and participate.

That meeting was the beginning of something that went beyond what any of us had envisioned. The board of TWS had certainly not made any plans as far as coordinating a camp or action beyond the initial three days. We were fortunate that there were people available to create a continuity, and our diversity brought great strength to the blockade.

The sandy shoreline of Wakimika served as our home. A pair of majestic pines were the focal and spiritual centre of the camp, reminding us of our purpose, supporting our clothesline, and acting as a tower for the radio antenna. From there the camp spread out through the cedars and colorful hardwoods.

After the first few days of the action, we realized that the government was not prepared to call off the bulldozers, and we would be in for a long struggle. We moved our tents back off the beach, as the sand was getting into everything and the wind was often harsh. We raised a tarp shelter over our cooking fire, and built picnic tables from wood brought in on the planes. From the beginning we maintained a latrine far back from the lake, and people took on the task of digging new holes as needed. There was a food supply tent that was kept in order by diligent workers. And there was the Warm Tent, complete with a small woodstove, where evening discussions took place, where tentless visitors could find a bed, and where we could shelter together from the cold and stormy weather that came more frequently as the autumn passed.

"Surviving the elements, minimizing our impact on the site, and enjoying the rugged beauty of our temporary home drew us together as a community."

Although many of the people who joined the blockade were not from the area, many had some history there—a family cottage, a childhood experience at a Temagami camp, memories of an extraordinary canoe trip through the crystal clear waterways. There were a few TWS employees whose duties soon involved helping to sustain the camp, but beyond these individuals, everyone was a volunteer. People came literally from all over the world to take part in an action that empowered all those who took the long trip into the bush.

The northerners on the blockade knew that fighting for sustainability was the key to giving us a future and providing for our children. It was our role to share the truths of northern existence, where activists must live and work without anonymity—a fact that keeps us in constant check as to how far we can go without being alienated from our neighbors. In the case of Temagami—an issue that had often been dismissed locally as southern interference in northern affairs—the show of support by northerners at the blockade was important both to the participants and to the general public.

There were people who made a quick trip in to the camp and then out from the road via the police vans; others who stayed for a few days or a week; and others who gave up jobs, relationships and other commitments in order to participate in what was to be for many a life-changing experience. All brought skills and personal power to share. We all gained invaluable insights, strong friendships, personal courage, and the knowledge of how empowering it is to take collective action for social and ecological justice. Surviving the elements, minimizing our impact on the site, and enjoying the rugged beauty of our temporary home drew us together as a community.

Anyone who has lived with a large group of people knows the struggles that can erupt in creating unity amongst diversity. Anyone who has been involved in political action recognizes the stress that outside pressures can put on group activities, and the frustration with political self-interest and the fickleness of the media. Anyone who has spent time in the northern bush knows that even though it is a beautiful place to be, it requires stamina and clear thinking to survive in it safely.

All of these conditions existed for the blockade community. We were a group of diverse people living in a primitive camp in the bush, doing political action with no guidebook to direct us. On top of this, the majority of the participants changed daily, mixing those of us who lived there for the better part of the seven weeks with newcomers, some of whom had never even been in the bush before. We had to think globally and act locally, try to live frugally, learn to share the chores as well as our feelings, and deal with problems of communications and transportation.

Because of our location—a day-long canoe trip or a series of three boat trips and two portages from the end of an hour's drive up a gravel road, or else a half-hour ride in a bush plane—bringing people into the camp was always an adventure. If the weather was fine, it was a pleasant journey beneath blue skies on friendly lakes. But when the weather was nasty, people at either end of the journey feared for the comfort and safety of the travellers. We watched planes take off and land in white-capped waves, and wondered how long our luck would hold.

Somehow it did: we only had two vehicle accidents on the road and no major water accidents, although we did cause serious injury to some boats. Our supplies also came in by boat or plane, so we were always anxious for fresh food—and maybe some chocolate almonds if we were lucky!

Our radio contact was with our friends Hap and Trudy at Smoothwater Outfitters near the village of Temagami, who gave their home, their business, their outfitting equipment and their own energies to the blockade, an extraordinary donation that we couldn't have functioned without. Smoothwater became our communications center, where blockaders came to link up with the transportation, and where our radio messages could be relayed by phone to the rest of the world. We tried to stay in touch with TWS in Toronto and with Northwatch in

North Bay, but radio contact was often interrupted due to technical difficulties or bad weather, and, knowing that our radio was most likely being monitored, we didn't want to use it to discuss our plans openly.

As in any situation where there are poor communications, we suffered deeply for it. The people in the bush lost track of what was happening in the outside world and would fall into a group depression until news arrived. Often it would take only one person's fears to dissolve the armour of resolve that kept the group healthy. I would leave one day and everyone would be feeling strong and united. When I returned a couple of days later, an almost visible black cloud would be hovering over the Warm Tent. The best medicine seemed to be news from beyond the camp. We would then spend the evening discussing the support we were receiving outside, our fears, what actions we could effect, and why we were still there. Then we would form a new resolve and laugh at our paranoia.

"We were also trying to come to terms with our relationship with the Teme Augama Anishnabai, the Deep Water People, on whose land we were squatting. ... we were forced to recognize our differing perspectives and learn to demonstrate respect for their judgments."

The second weekend of the blockade, local supporters of the logging industry advertised a "baseball game" that they were going to play with the blockaders. A bus load of angry counter-protesters was expected to drive in as far as possible and then walk down the cleared right-of-way, or slash, to meet us. When we heard about this at our end we quickly decided to stay put at the camp, the road work being a safe distance away through the bush and up the slash. With a cold early blizzard blowing, we were thankful not to have to assume our posts up on the road that day. Instead, the thirty or so people there prepared a wonderful meal and danced under the canvas shelter to music from the radio. Meanwhile, supporters on the outside had no way of knowing that we were safe.

Even on the blockade itself, the people who remained in camp every day often had little news about the events that were unfolding at the road construction site. As preparations for most actions took place in the night and the main event of the day would happen very early, we often wouldn't have news of arrests or successful work blockages until late in the morning. Many blockaders will remember the anxious hours spent waiting for news from the action, news from the outside, news from travellers that we knew were out on the lakes somewhere.

We were also trying to come to terms with our relationship with the Teme Augama Anishnabai, the Deep Water People, on whose land we were squatting. In our desire to support them in their struggle for justice, we were forced to recognize our differing perspectives and learn to demonstrate respect for their judgments. This respect would eventually cause our withdrawal from the bush when Chief Gary Potts announced the Band's intention to establish their own blockade. They demanded that all visitors to their land—the police, the construction company, and the TWS blockaders—leave n'Daki Menan. We were the only group who heeded their wishes.

We had strong support from a wide variety of sources. TWS acquired a huge debt in maintaining the camp. Smoothwater and some other camps donated equipment which we put to extreme use. Individuals donated boats that were definitely in worse repair by the end of the two months. People up and down the highway from Kirkland Lake to New Liskeard to North Bay housed people, collected donated goods, and shuttled people from the police depots that had been set up specifically for the blockade.

Our camp community opened its arms to all who arrived, often completely unprepared for what they would find and shocked at how deep into the northern bush they had come. We held meetings each day for the new arrivals, to welcome them, invite their input and energies, explain the positions we had developed as we adapted to each new situation, and collectively plan the next day's actions. We never pushed people to go to the road and risk arrest; that was their own decision. We were thankful for new skills and perspectives and for the return of familiar faces, as there were many who returned several times to the camp.

A recurring problem arose around people suspected of being plants from the police or agitators from the industry. We had every reason to believe that the police would plant people to find out what we were up to, and we also feared we could be set up for a serious charge. We had a difficult time coming to terms with our paranoia and learning to deal with these characters in a way that neither gave them too much information or access to our strategies, nor risked insulting them when our fears were unjustified. It was because of these fears, and the recognition of how disabling our paranoia was, that we created an inner circle of people that we knew personally and who were absolutely trustworthy.

At first we weren't comfortable with this, as it meant excluding some people from the planning process. There were few secrets, but just having the ability to discuss certain aspects of the actions with complete confidence was necessary to maintain our strength of mind. At times like this the needs of the community had to be put in perspective with the reason we were there—an illegal blockade of a road. The responsibility to protect those risking arrest was paramount. We would explain to new arrivals why we had created this inner circle, and very few had a problem with it.

"We struggled with how the needs of the individual conflict with the good of the group, attempting to come to terms with how we sometimes unwittingly support traditional male/female roles, and how we could change."

It was clear that our presence in the bush ignited the fires throughout the province and kept the heat on the government. A rally in Toronto in the sixth week of the blockade drew well over 1,000 people, yet the ten or so folks left at the camp passed that day listening to the sounds of the bulldozers they couldn't stop, and mourning the news that the natives had lost another injunction. We were running out of ways to halt the machines, and were watching the numbers of supporters dwindling off, although still hardly a day passed in seven weeks that new people didn't arrive.

We watched our members fall sick with viruses, colds and exhaustion. People tended to be very kind to each other and tried to share all the duties, adapting daily to smaller numbers of healthy bodies, colder weather demanding more firewood, and diminishing food supplies demanding more creativity.

Obviously living a bush life didn't demand a dress code or clean hair, and for most of us this was wonderful. We had morning contests to see who could create the best sculpture out of their increasingly oiled hair. The lake kept us clean but ice was forming on it toward the end of the seven weeks. We built a sweat lodge for the occasional sweat that was always a strong emotional experience. And one enthusiastic participant brought in two 45gallon drums which we would fill with water and set upon a fire, to have the most luxurious hot tub under the stars that a person could want.

Towards the end of the blockade, we set up an auxiliary camp near the base of a big pine beside the slash. Connected by radio with the main camp, a half-hour's paddle away, we took turns providing on-site support for one amazing woman who lived in a treefort seventy feet up for eleven days and nights, until the construction crew was forced to move the road around the tree!

Two-year-old Asa, who was part of the community for most of the seven weeks, provided us all with a child's perspective when life got too serious. His parents brought the needs of their relationship to the camp and we dealt with conflict resolution and gender discrimination. Our attempts to share child care were difficult as Asa was still breastfeeding. We struggled with how the needs of the individual conflict with the good of the group, attempting to come to terms with how we sometimes unwittingly support traditional male/female roles, and how we could change.

"There were certain male personalities who came to the camp and could throw everyone into absolute emotional turmoil within an hour."

I believe it was the strong presence of women that kept the blockade not only sane but healthy and alive. From the beginning of the planning stages through to the end of the blockade, there were several women who held on to their principles in the face of severe conflict with many of the powerful male figures. If there had been fewer women and more alpha-type males present in the camp, it could have easily taken on a military character, insulted other egos, and possibly fallen apart in conflict.

The women believed in the process. We knew that whether we stopped the road or not, we would all gain if we proceeded with integrity, openness, humility, intelligence and humor. We realized that people are empowered by the chance to state their opinions without fear of ridicule, and within the framework of our guidelines for the action, we used consensus process. We protected the nonviolent nature of the blockade and through respect and humor kept a calm rhythm alive in our community.

But this was often very hard. There were certain male personalities who came to the camp and could throw everyone into absolute emotional turmoil within an hour. You could almost see them coming, waving a flag of male domination and testosterone. Yet even when we felt like telling someone to leave our happy home on the back of a raging bull, we knew it was important that we treat each person with respect and hear them out.

In general most of the men attempted to blend with the group. In fact, one group of men in their early twenties formed a solid core of the blockade community. They did much of the dangerous work of driving boats across cold waters in the falling dark by themselves. They brought their skills of canoeing and cooking blueberry crisp in reflector ovens and building treeforts while suspended by ropes high above the slash. For some of them it was not only their first political action but also their first real experience with strong-voiced feminists.

"I believe that the integrity with which we conducted the blockade also empowered the northern community to raise a common front against the next assault on their lives—Toronto's plans to ship its garbage north."

The women in the camp had a wonderful opportunity to teach these young men so much both by example and through conversation. Sexist language and actions were never tolerated, but the women also learned to approach conflict situations with patience and humor. I believe that the men on the blockade were enlightened by their relationships with these women through the power of open and friendly dialogue, and relationships of love and respect formed that exist amongst us all today.

The Temagami blockade brought to the forefront the issues of environmental and native rights, and represented the commitment that people had to nonviolent resistance. Even when we were no longer able to physically stop the machines, we kept our presence at the roadsite, and our collective voice continued to reverberate throughout the province.

I believe that the integrity with which we conducted the blockade also empowered the northern community to raise a common front against the next assault on their lives—Toronto's plans to ship its garbage north. Many people in the area who had never raised their voice in anger publicly on an environmental issue before, spoke up against this new threat.

The incredible support the blockade evoked was also a response to the powerful force that grew out of that camp community. The experience changed many of our lives and renewed our commitment to social change. After the blockade, several people made life decisions that chipped away at what is superfluous to our existence and confuses our priorities. Many others saw life in all its clarity and responded accordingly.

*

The ice crystallized on Wakimika Lake as we packed up the camp on November 10. After three days of planes not being able to fly due to icing on the wings, we finally had the last two hours of sunlight to get everything into the planes and get out of the bush. I don't think any of us really wanted to leave, as the camp had been our home for two months and we were amongst family. We had created a community of forest dwellers and now had to return to "real life."

Yet life had never been so real. We had laughed and sung and danced and talked and dreamt and argued and walked; we had shared victory and mourned defeat. That was what we had come there for; it was our human right to fight for social justice, our only arms the ones with which we hugged the trees.

The Goose Story

Anonymous

In the fall, when you see geese heading south for the winter, flying along in V-formation, think about what science has learned about why they fly that way. As each bird flaps her wings, she creates uplift for the bird immediately following her. By flying in a V-formation, the whole flock can fly at least seventy-one per cent farther than if each bird flew on her own. Perhaps people who share a common direction can get where they are going quicker and easier if they cooperate.

Whenever a goose falls out of formation, he feels the resistance of trying to go it alone, and quickly gets back into formation to take advantage of flying with the flock. If we have as much sense as a goose, we will work with others who are going the same way as we are.

When the lead goose gets tired, she rotates back in the wing and another goose flies on the point. It pays to take turns doing hard jobs for our group. The geese honk from behind to encourage those up front to keep up their speed.

Finally, (get this!) when a goose weakens or is wounded and falls out of formation, two geese fall out and follow him down to help and protect him. They stay with him until he is either able to fly or until he is dead, and then they set out on their own or with another formation until they catch up with the group. If we had the sense of a goose, we would stand by each other like that.

Resources

For further information about intentional communities, write:

Fellowship for Intentional Community
Center for Communal Studies
8600 University Boulevard
Evansville, IN 47712, USA

Federation for Egalitarian Communities
c/o East Wind Community
Tecumseh, MO 65760, USA

The *Directory of Intentional Communities* contains North American and international community listings, articles and resources, and can be obtained from:

Directory
c/o Sandhill Farm
Route 1, Box 155
Rutledge, MO 63563, USA